A PRACTICAL STEP-BY-STEP GUIDE

GROWING AND DISPLAYING BONSAI

A PRACTICAL STEP-BY-STEP GUIDE

GROWING AND DISPLAYING BONSAI

COLIN LEWIS
WITH PHOTOGRAPHS BY NEIL SUTHERLAND

This edition published in 2001 by Advanced Marketing, Bicester, Oxfordshire.

Produced by Salamander Books Limited,
8 Blenheim Court, Brewery Road,
London N7 9NT, United Kingdom
A member of the Chrysalis Group plc

Some of the material that appears in this book was previously published in *A Creative Step-by-step Guide to Growing and Displaying Bonsai*, also by Colin Lewis.

ISBN 1-90168-303-6

Printed and bound in Italy

CREDITS
Designed and edited by: FOCUS PUBLISHING, The Courtyard, 26 London Road, Sevenoaks, Kent TN13 1AP
Designers: Sam Hemphill, Philip Clucas
Editors: Guy Croton, Caroline Watson
Photographer: Neil Sutherland
Illustrator: Tim Heyward, courtesy of Bernard Thornton Artists
Editorial director: Will Steeds

THE AUTHOR
Colin Lewis admits to having spent much of his childhood in conversation withtrees. In 1974, he combined this affection for trees with his formal training as a designer, and began growing bonsai on the window-sill of his London apartment. In 1989, he travelled to Japan to study bonsai, and now regularly teaches and writes for magazines throughout Europe. He has exhibited trees at the Chelsea Flower Show, the National Bonsai Collection and the Annual Bonsai and Suiseki Exhibition in Osaka, Japan.

PHOTOGRAPHER
Neil Sutherland has more than 25 years' experience in a wide range of photographic fields, including still life, portraiture, reportage, natural history, cookery, landscape and travel. His work has been published in countless books and magazines throughout the world.

Half-title page, title page and contents page: All photographs by Neil Sutherland

Contents

WHAT IS A BONSAI?

The main aim of bonsai is to create a tree-like form in miniature. This can be anything from a precise replica of a classic parkland beech to the image of a gnarled and weather-beaten mountain-top juniper, which can be almost abstract in its design.

The two syllables of the Japanese word bonsai literally translate as 'a tree in a pot', but when combined they acquire an altogether grander meaning. A bonsai is a plant which is established in an aesthetically harmonious container, and has been subjected to a number of horticultural and sculptural techniques in order to create a tree-like image.

The pollarded willow is a familiar sight in northern Europe. This ten-inch high bonsai is pruned back annually, in exactly the same way as its full-sized counterpart.

A bonsai is not a naturally dwarfed variety, neither is it chemically treated to stop it growing larger. Its growth is not restricted by confining the roots in a pot, but by constant clipping and trimming. The size and shape are entirely determined by its keeper, whose horticultural and artistic skills also determine its eventual health and aesthetic quality.

HOW OLD IS A BONSAI?

A bonsai does not have to be old to be good. It is quite possible to create a delightful little tree in an afternoon, although until it is established in its pot it is not a true bonsai. Having said this, bonsai do improve with age. So over the years, with the right care and attention, a good bonsai can become a better bonsai. However, a poorly designed young tree can only become a poorly designed old tree, so it is essential to get the basic form right from the start.

ORIGINS

No-one knows exactly when the first bonsai was grown, but we do know that the ancient Chinese cultivated miniature landscapes in shallow containers. Complete with trees,

The Japanese characters for 'bonsai' *are identical to the Chinese for* 'pun–sai'. *Both translate as 'a tree in a pot'.*

'The classic pine'. An illustration from a Japanese bonsai instruction manual, published in 1829.

A first-day cover, produced in commemoration of the World Bonsai Convention, held in Omiya, Japan in 1989. This indicates the significance of bonsai in modern Japanese culture.

rocks and mosses, these landscapes, or *penjing*, were the forerunners of bonsai.

Single tree plantings came later, but exactly when is unclear. These were called *pun-sai*, the Chinese root of the Japanese word bonsai. When the Chinese invaded Japan in the Middle Ages they introduced the Buddhist religion. The monks at that time were custodians of all forms of cultural heritage and took with them their written language, their art and their bonsai. At that time all bonsai were created from ancient stunted trees collected from the mountains, where their constant battle with the harsh environment had restricted their size and given them gnarled and twisted shapes. The tenacity of these trees was held in such reverence that they were deemed to possess spiritual qualities which would be inherited by their owners.

It was not until this century that the ordinary citizen began to practise bonsai, by which time it had become a highly refined and structured discipline. Such was the commitment of the dedicated bonsai artist that a group of them decided to further their art by forming the 'bonsai village', Omiya, which is now an outer suburb of Tokyo and a mecca for bonsai enthusiasts the world over.

A commercial bonsai 'farm' near Takamatsu, Japan, where field after field of developing bonsai can be seen. These black pines are about twelve years old.

BONSAI: ART OR HORTICULTURE?

At its highest level, bonsai is pure sculpture; living plant material providing the medium while horticulture provides the means by which the artist creates. However, the pleasure each individual gains from growing bonsai will vary according to their reasons for taking up the hobby.

A keen gardener may regard bonsai as a new horticultural challenge, as might a plant lover living in a flat with only a balcony for a garden. On the other hand, someone from an artistic background may discover in bonsai the one medium through which they can achieve creative fulfilment.

As a beginner, you will probably be more concerned with the horticulture and a little nervous of some of the techniques. But within a short time you will gain confidence as you see your trees respond to the treatment. As confidence grows you will try new ideas. Some of these experiments will succeed but some will inevitably fail. However, from each failure you learn a little more, until you eventually understand what nature will, and will not, allow you to do.

INSPIRATIONS

We are all surrounded by trees of one sort or another, and these naturally form the basis of all bonsai artists' inspiration. But just looking at trees is not enough – you have to really see them in order subconsciously to analyse their structure, so you can reproduce more authentic images in miniature.

The Japanese are almost fanatic about shaping trees. This black pine is growing next to a footpath in Kyoto. Each shoot is individually pruned every two or three years.

You don't have to travel far to find inspiration. Notice how the branch structure on this English oak echoes that of the Japanese pine shown above.

Ask an eight-year-old to draw a tree and you will probably be presented with a straight brown trunk topped by a solid green circle. The child will know that the trunk is grey rather than brown, and that a tree has visible branches supporting a crown which will certainly not be round. Even so, children lack the analytical ability necessary to transfer this knowledge onto paper.

Most adults do have this ability, but learning how to use it in the bonsai context can take a little practice. Spend as much time as possible studying trees, single specimens or groups, especially during the winter months when the structures of deciduous varieties are clearly visible. You will notice how the branches on younger trees tend to grow upwards while those on older trees are more horizontal. If you look up into the canopy of old pines you will find the branches twist and turn in all directions, reflecting the influence of the weather on the supple young shoots. You will also find natural jins and sharis and will be able to trace how they were formed years ago. You don't have to travel to the wild mountain sides to see these things, they are all around us, in our parks and gardens, and form the basis for many bonsai styles.

But if you do go further afield, you will be in for a real treat. Mountain trees grow in thin, poor soil and are exposed to high winds and storms. Their constant battle for survival imparts to them immense character: twisted and gnarled branches, roots exposed by soil erosion and trunks stripped almost bare of their bark. Here we find the inspiration behind styles like windswept, root-over-rock and literati and cascade.

PHOTOGRAPHY

Wherever you travel, take a camera with you to record what you see. You will soon build up a valuable reference library of photographs which will be a great help when working on difficult new material.

It is also a good idea to create photographic records of your bonsai as they develop over the years. The changes may well be too subtle to notice as you inspect each tree daily, but when you look at pictures taken two or three years ago, the differences can be quite dramatic. Keep your pictures in an album and record the date they were taken.

This Chinese Juniper, growing in a Japanese landscape garden, is hundreds of years old. Its heavy, gnarled old trunk displays a wealth of natural sharis and jins.

The eight-inch tall Japanese larch, and the dwarf chamaecyparis *on the left, are planted in vertical channels cut into the back of the rock*

Left: *Two pieces of metamorphic sandstone from Wales form the container of this* cascade style ishitsuki *bonsai. The image is one of an ancient larch struggling for survival as it clings to a mountain precipice.*

Colonies of lichen make the rock appear ancient and weathered

A tiny thyme planted at the base of the cliff completes the picture

SIZE AND AGE

One of the first questions people ask on their initial encounter with bonsai is, 'How old is it?' They are naturally fascinated by these ancient-looking specimens, and the thought that they have been cared for by successive generations of devoted artists.

In many cases, especially with collected wild trees, it is impossible to know the exact age, one can only guess. As one famous bonsai master says: 'You should never ask a beautiful woman her age'.

Sadly, a few unscrupulous dealers cash in on this fascination with the age of bonsai, and exaggerate the ages of their stock. If the image is one of an eighty-year-old tree, they will claim this to be the true age. Factors such as immature bark texture and unhealed pruning wounds expose their deceit.

Once you have grown a few bonsai yourself, you will come to realise just how unimportant the true age really is compared with the apparent age. More significant is the length of time the tree has been in training as a bonsai. Even this is of secondary importance when compared to the beauty of form, colour and texture.

Size is another factor whose importance is frequently over-rated. It is often assumed that the larger the bonsai, the older, and therefore the better, it is. This is not true. It is also often assumed that bigger bonsai are technically and aesthetically more difficult to create and maintain. Also not true.

This tiny shohin *is only six-and-a-half inches tall from the rim of the pot. It started its bonsai career as a tiny shoot bearing only five leaves, and has been in training for a total of eighteen years. The surface roots and trunk formation are excellent, and the branch structure, which is the result of many years of constant pinching and detailed fine wiring, compares favourably with any of the finest large bonsai.*

In fact, a small or *shohin* bonsai requires more ingenuity and patience to create, because the artist has to work with fewer elements, yet still has to aspire to the same aesthetic standards which apply to larger trees.

A shohin bonsai also demands far more constant attention to maintain. The pots dry out quicker, shoots outgrow the design more often and, if left to grow for too long, will sap the energy from the fine twigs, causing them to wither and die.

This medium-size bonsai stands eleven inches tall from the rim of the pot. It was collected eleven years ago and spent the next two years in the flower border, where it received some initial training. The larger pot has helped to speed up its development.

At this scale, fine twigs develop rapidly

This awkward kink in the trunk was already established when the tree was dug up

The superb surface root formation was helped by the time spent in open ground

At this scale the foliage remains coarse, even though the tree was leaf-pruned a month before this photograph was taken (see page 60)

Young shoots are still being allowed to develop into mature branches

At twenty-two inches tall, this bonsai is quite large, although by no means the largest I have seen. It was collected only six years ago from a roadside verge, and was planted directly into a bonsai container. Originally, the tree was seven feet tall, and was reduced on collection, using the technique outlined on page 38.

The one-sided root formation is typical of collected suckers at this size. It is too well established to change at this stage

THE BASICS

HOW A BONSAI GROWS: ROOT TO LEAF

Your bonsai is the result of an interaction between you and nature, and the success of everything you do relies upon the tree's natural response to your actions.

In order to get the best out of your hobby, it is important to have at least a basic understanding of how a tree works.

ROOTS

Roots have three functions. One, quite simply, is to hold the tree steady in the soil. This is performed by thick, strong roots which radiate from the base of the trunk. The second function is to store nutrients during the dormant period, ready for use when growth resumes in spring. The third function is to absorb water and nutrients, via tiny, single-cell protrusions called root hairs, which clothe the young roots as they grow.

THE TRUNK AND BRANCHES

Like roots, the trunk and branches also perform three functions. The first is structural, supporting the branches and foliage. The second, also like roots, is to store nutrients until needed.

The third function is to carry water and nutrients from one part of the tree to another, either side of the cambium layer.

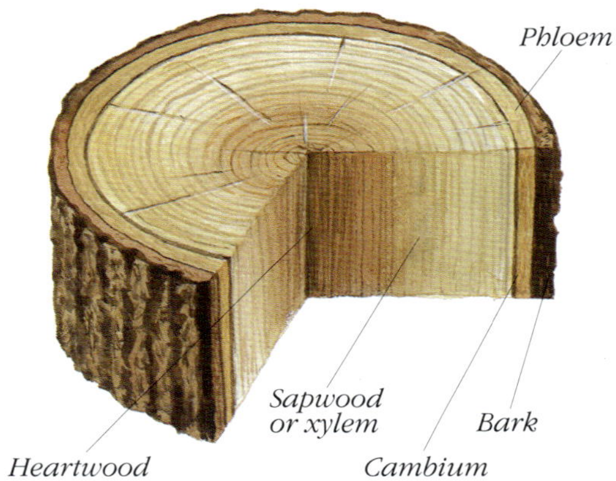

1 *This cross-section shows the different layers that make up the trunk of a tree. The heartwood is essentially dead and acts in a structural capacity.*

ROOT PROBLEMS

Apart from insect attack, the only serious problem you will need to cope with is root rot, which is easier to prevent than cure. Ensure that the roots remain healthy at all times. Use a free-draining soil with plenty of air spaces. Avoid over-feeding. Roots absorb water by osmosis, whereby a weak solution passes through a membrane (the wall of the root) towards a stronger solution. If the water in the soil contains a stronger solution of nutrients than that in the root, water will pass from the root back into the soil, damaging the roots and depriving the tree of water.

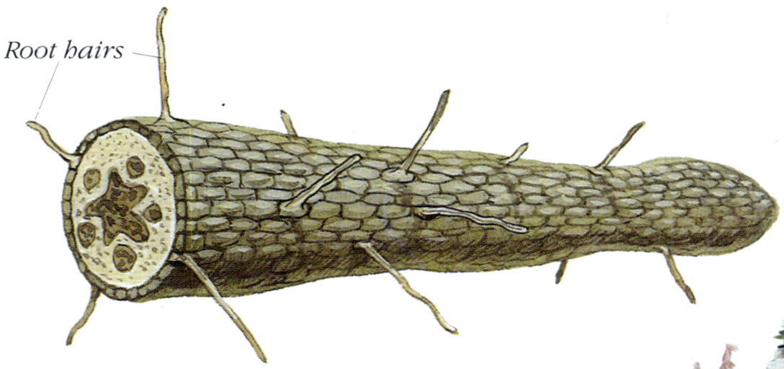

2 *The growing tip of a root, showing the single-cell root hairs and the main transport vessels.*

THE CAMBIUM LAYER

This is really the 'magic' part of the tree, responsible for controlling the growth. It is a single-cell layer just beneath the bark and appears green when the bark is scraped away.

During the growing season, the cambium layer produces a new layer of tissue on either side. On the inside is the sapwood, or xylem, through which the water is transported from the roots throughout the tree.

On the outside the new layer is called the phloem, and this is responsible for distributing the sugars produced in the leaves to other parts of the tree.

The cambium layer is also responsible for producing new roots in cuttings and air layers, and adventitious buds, as well as the tissue which heals over wounds.

FOLIAGE

All leaves are basically food factories, using light as a catalyst to convert water supplied by the roots and carbon dioxide absorbed from the air into sugars, in a process called photosynthesis. These sugars provide growth energy to the plant.

This gorgeous azalea (Rhododendron indicum 'Eikan') *is kept in vibrant health by its owner, Ruth Stafford-Jones.*

During the day the leaves 'breathe in' through small pores called stomata, and at night they expel the excess oxygen and other gaseous by-products. They also allow water to evaporate through the surface in order to keep up a constant flow.

Some trees' leaves have a waxy coating which will help conserve moisture during the winter, when the roots are frozen and unable to function. This coating also serves to prevent snow and ice adhering to the surfaces and suffocating the tree.

3 *Cross section of a leaf from a broadleaved tree. Each leaf is a tiny 'food factory', providing nourishment for the plant during the summer months.*

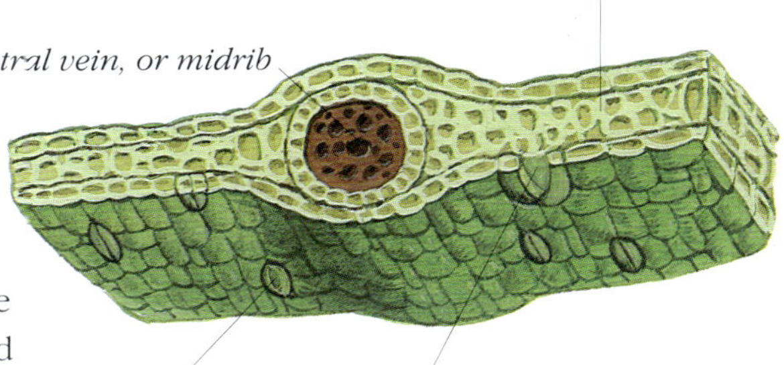

HOW A BONSAI GROWS: BUDS

Buds come in many different shapes and sizes, but they all have one thing in common. They all contain an entire new shoot, minutely formed and tightly packed within a protective sheath of scales.

To get an idea of what a bud looks like inside, just cut a savoy cabbage in half. You will clearly see the foreshortened shoot and folded leaves, with the dark outer leaves serving as scales. It is hard to imagine how so much could be contained in a bud which may be no bigger than a pinhead.

1 *Delicate elm buds unfurl to reveal minute, bright green leaves.*

- Terminal or apical buds are formed at the tips of the current year's shoots and are usually the largest since they contain next year's extension growth. These are often flanked by smaller axillary buds.
- Axillary buds are formed along the length of the shoot, in each leaf axil (the point where the leaf stem, or petiole, joins the shoot), or in the axils of the bud scales. They will either produce the shorter side shoots next year or remain dormant.
- Dormant buds are generally axillary buds which failed to open in the year following their formation. They can remain, barely visible, for several years until they are stimulated into growth by pruning, feeding or increased light levels.
- Adventitious buds can emerge anywhere on old wood, around pruning cuts or even on roots. They are the tree's response to improved conditions or its method of regeneration after loss of foliage mass. Adventitious buds tend to produce vigorous, sappy shots.

CUT-AWAY BUD

Left: *A bud is in fact an entire new shoot, complete with its own apical and axillary buds. It is tightly compressed and protected all over by scales.*

2 *Spruce (illustrated) and needle-leaved junipers produce masses of buds. They open quickly, exposing tight clusters of needles, which rapidly extend into soft, tender shoots.*

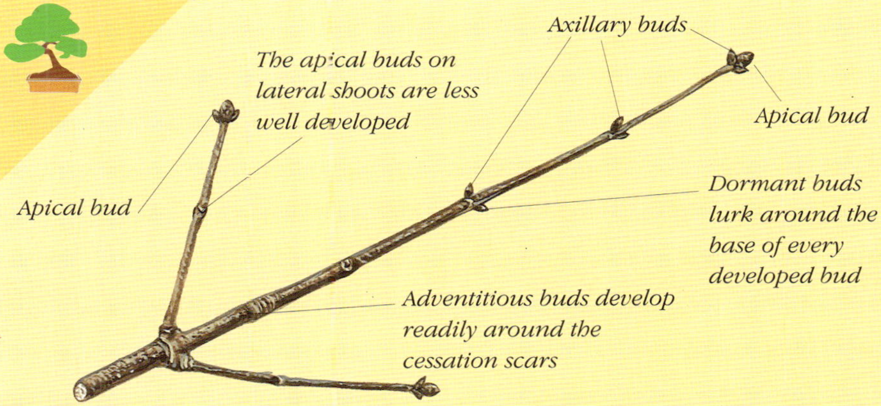

Above: *In winter, many trees can be identified by their buds. However, all deciduous shoots bear apical and axillary buds, as well as showing 'cessation scars'.*

With Japanese red maples, the colour in spring is every bit as impressive as it is in autumn. The leaves are smaller, and much brighter.

4 *The scales on maple buds peel back so the brightly coloured leaves develop. At this stage they are very prone to frost and aphid damage.*

5 *Pine buds don't open in the same way as other trees. They elongate, shedding the papery scales as they do so.*

3 *Larch buds lose their papery scales to expose tiny 'shaving brushes' of new needles. Larch shoots emerge from the centres of these clusters, retaining the mass of needles at the base, providing dormant buds. If the buds are dislodged at this stage, they cannot form dormant buds around the base, so treat with care.*

6 *These fat prominent buds at the tips of azalea shoots are in fact flower buds. The growth buds are nestled in the axils of the leaves just below them.*

BUYING BONSAI

Many newcomers to bonsai begin by being tempted to buy one at a garden centre. This is not always a good idea: the so-called bonsai offered for sale at garden centres are invariably tropical species from the Far or Middle East which may be suffering from neglect.

Tropical species cannot tolerate our climate, so they must be kept inside for most of the year. This is fine if you can provide a controlled environment, which is not easy. If garden centre plants have been in stock for a long time, they may not have received this basic care. So, if you are intent on growing bonsai indoors, go to a reputable specialist nursery, whose plants will be well cared for and whose staff will be able to offer good advice.

The same advice applies to buying hardy species. Specialist growers know their stuff, so benefit from their experience. Meanwhile, the following points will help you to get the best value for money.

PRICE

- Bonsai are expensive because it takes time to create them by hand, and they are transported half way round the world. Less than a reasonable price will only buy a 'half finished' bonsai, requiring several years' work to refine.

HEALTH

- It is best to buy any plant during the growing season so you can be sure it is alive

WHAT *NOT* TO LOOK FOR!

Neither of these plants could be called a bonsai. The pine *(above)* is a three-year-old seedling which was pruned once at the end of its second year. The grower wired the trunk to make it look authentic, without altering the shape.

The little Japanese maple *(right)* is four years old. Its trunk has been shaped with wire by somebody who has clearly never seen a real tree! There is no way this misshapen freak could be turned into a bonsai.

and healthy. If you buy in winter, scratch the bark a little: if it is green underneath the plant is alive, if not, it is dead.

- Avoid plants with die back, damaged leaves etc., which may be symptoms of disease.
- Check the tree is firm in its pot.
- Check the soil. This should be loose and porous, moist but not waterlogged.

APPEARANCE

- The surface roots should look natural as they emerge from the trunk. The trunk should have a natural shape and taper, with no unsightly scars or graft unions. Avoid bonsai with exaggerated spirals and hairpin bends.
- The branches should be evenly distributed around the trunk, the lower ones being thicker than those at the top.
- Make sure there are no wire marks on the trunk or branches or, worse still, that there is no wire embedded in the bark.

AFTERCARE

- Always ask the nurseryman about the tree's specific horticultural requirements such as watering, feeding, winter protection and so on, and try to find out when it was last repotted so you know when next to tackle this task. If you take the trouble to ask lots of questions when you are buying your bonsai, you are much less likely to experience problems later on.

Above: *When you see trees presented like this, you can be fairly confident you are getting good value. They are all healthy and weed-free, and the fertiliser pellets on each pot show they are well cared for.*

Japanese cypress (Cryptomeria Japonica). *This magnificent bonsai is very ancient indeed, well over a hundred years old. Its trunk is hollow all the way up and the branches are by now very brittle.*

GARDEN CENTRE STOCK

The real essence of bonsai is creating your own, and the most readily available raw material is to be found in garden centres. There is a bewildering range of species and sizes to choose from, which only serves to make the decision more difficult.

The following points will help you make a sensible choice and avoid wasting your money on inappropriate garden centre plants.

WHAT SPECIES?

- Deciduous or conifer? Conifers make more 'instant' bonsai and deciduous species take longer to develop, but the latter will reward you with changes in colour and form.
- Avoid slow growing or dwarf varieties because they can take a longer time to respond to training.
- If you want a flowering species, choose one which flowers on the previous year's wood.
- Test the branches to check that they are supple enough to be shaped by wiring.
- Finally, decide on a variety which already has smallish leaves or needles and shows a readiness to produce buds on older wood.

FINAL CHOICE

Once you decide on the species, you need to select the plant with the most potential.

- Examine each plant carefully. Expose the surface roots to see if they appear natural.
- There should be plenty of low branches which still bear foliage close to the trunk.
- Don't assume that the existing trunk line will necessarily be the final one, or that the new bonsai will be the same size as the raw material. These options should be carefully considered at your leisure.

This little azalea was chosen for its superb root spread. It took only three years to reach this stage.

SUITABLE GARDEN CENTRE SPECIES

Some of the most reliable species with a proven record of suitability.

Acer – palmatum, Japonicum, (maples)
Azalea (botanically *Rhododendron)*
Berberis
Betula (birches)
Buxus (box)
Carpinus (hornbeam)
Cedrus (cedar – *brevifolia* is best)
Chaenomeles (quince)
Chamaecyparis (dwarf varieties are best)
Cotoneaster
Cratagus (hawthorn)
Cryptomeria
Fagus (beech)
Juniperus (all types)
Larix (larches)
Ligustrum (privet)
Lonicera nitida (hedge honeysuckle)
Picea (spruces)
Pinus (pines)
Potentilla
Prunus (flowering cherries)
Pyracantha
Spirea
Taxus (yew)
Ulmus (elms)
Wisteria
Zelkova

PLANTS TO BE AVOIDED

1 *At first you may be tempted by 'unusual' trunk shapes like this. But in the case of this plant, unusual means unnatural and it would never make a good bonsai.*

2 *Avoid older garden centre plants that are grafted onto sturdier root stocks, causing an unsightly swelling.*

3 *The odd weed shows that the plant has become established in the pot, but growth like this liverwort indicates poor drainage and unhealthy roots.*

4 *Good surface roots are essential in bonsai. Don't be tempted by bizarre root formations like this; they may seem interesting at first, but ultimately you will regret the purchase.*

5 *At first sight this dwarf cotoneaster seems ideal for bonsai. Closer inspection reveals that all the branches emerge straight from the soil and there is no trunk, making it useless.*

Propagation From Seed

If you have the patience there is nothing more rewarding than growing bonsai from seed, regardless of whether you intend to train it from scratch or grow the plant on to form larger raw material.

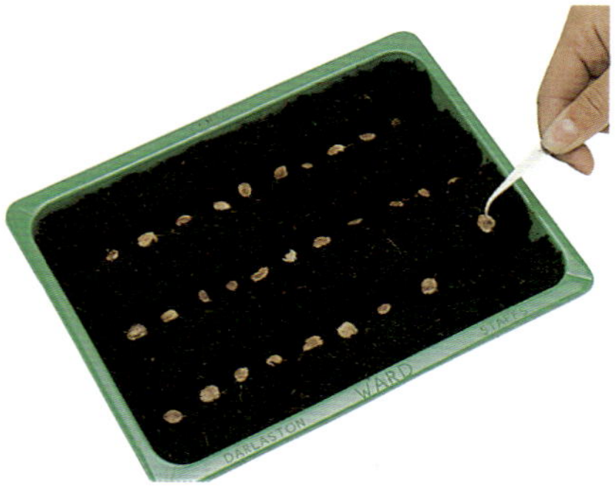

1 *Having cleaned your seeds, space them out evenly on a layer of fine compost in a seed tray. Hard seeds germinate better if the shells are chipped with a sharp knife.*

2 *Cover the seeds with a layer of compost, to a depth of roughly the thickness of the seeds. Don't press this down – leave it loose so that the seeds can breathe.*

Sowing seed for bonsai is basically carried out in the same way as for other purposes, but extra care is needed when pricking out seedlings.

- Before buying your seeds make sure the species is suitable *(see page 25)*.
- Use a sandier than normal soil, with no added fertiliser.
- Seeds with hard cases will germinate quicker if the shell is cracked or slit.
- The seeds of most hardy species need to be stratified before they will germinate. This involves exposing them to periods of low temperature, either outside or in a refrigerator for a few weeks.
- If you germinate your seeds indoors, harden them off gradually before siting them permanently outside.
- The seeds of some species, for example hornbeam and hawthorn, may take two years to germinate, so be patient.

3 *The seed tray should be watered with a spray. Adding a copper-based fungicide such as Chestnut compound helps prevent decay as well as 'damping off' the new seedlings.*

4 *Cover the seed tray, leaving the ventilation holes fully open. Place the tray outside, where the seeds will be subjected to natural changes in temperature.*

5 *Once the seedlings have their first true leaves, gently tease them out. Hold the leaves, not the stem.*

6 *Use a sharp sterile blade to cut through the tap root, leaving enough side roots to sustain the seedling.*

7 *When planting the seedlings in their growing pots, spread the roots radially from the stem. This is the first, essential step in bonsai training, ensuring a good root formation for the future.*

8 *Cover the roots with bonsai soil. Don't press the soil down as this may damage the tender young roots. Water gently and place the seedlings in a sheltered spot until new growth appears.*

Even after many generations, the importance of spreading the seedling's roots is clear

This massive, informal upright Japanese maple is one of the finest trees ever to leave Japan. It is curious to think that it was once a tiny seedling.

CUTTINGS

The advantage of propagating from cuttings of any type is that you can reproduce the exact characteristics of the parent plant, whereas plants grown from seed may vary. There are three types of cutting appropriate for bonsai: softwood, hardwood and root cuttings.

This little Cornish elm started as a root cutting nine years ago. The trunk was later hollowed out to give a really ancient appearance.

Softwood cuttings use new growth as the name implies. These should be taken in early summer, and need to be kept in an enclosed, humid atmosphere until they have taken root.

Hardwood cuttings use mature growth and are taken in the autumn, usually using shoots which have grown that year.

Root cuttings are suitable for species which naturally throw up shoots, or suckers, from the roots. They can be taken any time between November and April, using roots up to three inches thick.

3 *Commercial propagators are ideal. They have clear covers with controlled ventilation. Make your own by placing a plastic bag over a pot.*

1 *Softwood cuttings are taken in May and June. The lower leaves and the growing tips are cut off using a very sharp blade.*

2 *Handle the cuttings carefully, and insert them into sandy compost to a depth equal to about a third of their length. It is not necessary to use hormone treatment, although spraying them with systemic fungicide will help prevent decay, thus improving results.*

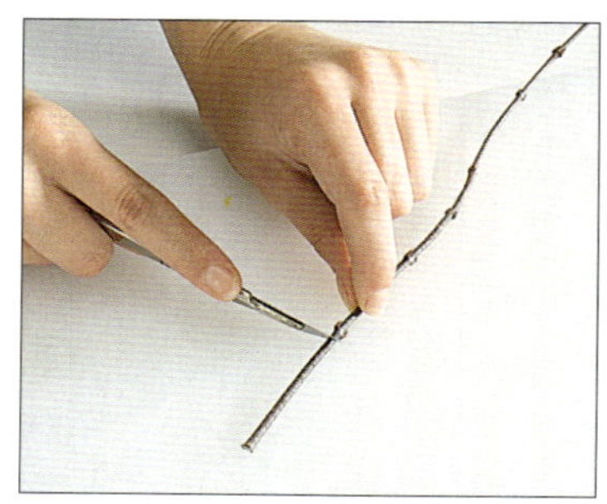

4 *There are two types of hardwood cuttings: nodal, and heel cuttings. Nodal cuttings should be cut cleanly with a sharp knife, just below a leaf node, or axillary bud, as shown.*

5 *When taking heel cuttings, pull the shoot away from its parent, retaining a sliver of bark, or heel. Trim the heel with a sharp knife.*

6 *Plant the cuttings to a depth of at least half their length, either in open ground or in a deep pot. Make the holes with a dibber to avoid damaging the ends of the cuttings.*

7 *When trimming root cuttings, use a very sharp blade as their soft bark crushes easily. Leaving a few feeder roots will help the cutting on its way.*

8 *For single-tree styles, the root cutting should be planted vertically, making sure it is the right way up!*

9 *For clump or raft styles, the root cuttings should be planted on their sides. Many new shoots will be produced.*

Chinese Juniper Cuttings

Chinese juniper cuttings generally root very easily, although they can take up to a year, so patience is needed. Take shoots of approximately three inches in length from last year's growth in June and then prepare them as shown, using a sharp scalpel. Be careful not to crush or damage the cuttings as you hold them still whilst preparing their ends.

AIR LAYERS

Most gardens will have a few shrubs or a hedge which has been regularly clipped over the years. This naturally produces areas where there are many small and interestingly-shaped branches bearing a network of small twigs.

It takes little imagination to see how good some of these little branches and twigs would look in pots after a little training – if only they had roots! If you're lucky you might have a flowering cherry, quince or pyracantha.

Spruce, cypresses, yew and junipers all work well, although pines don't co-operate. Most deciduous species will layer successfully but some take longer than others.

Air layering is a technique which enables you to induce roots to emerge exactly at the point you want them. It is like taking a cutting without actually severing the branch from its parent plant until the roots have grown.

This technique also comes in useful when you have an 'ex-bonsai' which has become so overgrown that it needs to be cut right back and have new branches grown on from scratch. By air layering the old branches you can use them to create more bonsai.

The best time to tackle this technique is early to mid-summer, as soon as the leaves have fully hardened. It is a good idea to give the tree a dose of fertiliser high in phosphates before you start to get it in the mood for making roots and remember never to let the polythene-covered moss dry out.

1 *Make two cuts round the trunk, and then another one vertically. On each occasion cut right through to the wood.*

2 *Peel away the bank of bark and scrape away every trace of cambium.*

3 *Take a strip of clear polythene and tie it tightly an inch below the wound. Leave a small overlap.*

5 *Once the roots have begun to turn brown, the branch can be severed below the polythene. Gently peel away the plastic. Take care not to damage the very delicate roots. If you allow the moss to fall away it will tear the roots.*

4 *Fill the polythene with fresh, moist sphagnum moss – the type sold by florists for hanging baskets – then tie the polythene loosely at the top. Keep the moss moist and inspect frequently until new roots are visible.*

Below: *These radial roots are typical of the kind of structure which can be achieved by air layering. The trick is to layer early in the year to give the new roots time to establish properly before winter.*

6 *Place the undisturbed root ball in a deep pot filled with fresh soil. Don't press down on the tender roots. Trim all long shoots to reduce demand on the new roots and put the new tree in a sheltered spot for a few weeks. Spray daily.*

GROWING YOUR OWN

Two of the most desirable features in any bonsai are mature bark and pronounced taper of the trunk. These properties are always difficult, and often impossible, to achieve when a tree has spent all its life growing slowly in the confines of a shallow bonsai pot.

1 *In full leaf this Siberian elm was just a bush, but in winter the trunk's potential can clearly be seen. Once dug, all the soil should be washed away from the roots with a hose.*

Traditionally, the most revered specimens were created from stunted plants collected from the mountains of Japan. But nowadays, to do this would be highly irresponsible almost anywhere in the world and certainly illegal in most western countries.

The only satisfactory solution is to grow your own raw material in a way which produces all the desirable characteristics in as short a time as possible. To do this you need to encourage the lower branches to grow in order to thicken the lower part of the trunk. If the base of the trunk is mulched with straw or leaf mould the bark will swell and crack, making it look even older.

The result is a heavy trunk with considerable taper, flaky bark and many old scars – all the characteristics of great age.

This technique of growing raw material is ideal for most

This massive azalea has been grown in open ground since 1952. It has been growing in a container for three years and is already taking shape nicely.

Azaleas grow very slowly. A trunk like this can take a very long time to form

2 *Every branch and shoot is cut off, leaving just the basic trunk. Prune the top branches selectively so you leave a uniform taper.*

3 *Cut the roots as far back as you can, but leave a few finer roots to sustain the plant. Use a sharp saw, as the roots will easily tear.*

5 *The tree should be placed in a polytunnel until new growth is established. This can take time, and the new growth may not appear until mid-summer or beyond.*

deciduous species, but not suitable for conifers since they will not regenerate growth once all the foliage-bearing branches have been removed.

When growing conifers in open ground prune back as hard as you can every two years, while still leaving some foliage on each branch. Each spring pinch out about half of every new 'candle' as soon as they are big enough to handle. This will produce masses of branches and shoots to choose from when you eventually come to style the tree.

The drastic root pruning shown here is successful with most elms and trident maple. With other species it is advisable to reduce the roots in stages during successive springs, repotting into a small container each time.

4 *Plant the trunk in a generous sized container filled with good bonsai soil. Cover the remaining roots well to conserve moisture.*

FIRST STEPS: CUTTINGS

Seedlings and cuttings are free and easy to come by, so they are ideal material for your first attempts at creating bonsai. If the result is not too good it doesn't really matter; you will probably have other plants ready to replace the initial failure.

A good result with cuttings means that you will have a bonsai that will improve as time goes by with the right care and attention.

We have repotted this cutting to complete the demonstration. You should ideally wait until the following spring, to allow the plant time to regain strength.

Whatever species you choose, seedling or cutting, the plant must be growing vigorously before you attempt any pruning or wiring.

For this sequence we selected a two-year-old cutting of a juniper, *Juniperus squamata meyerii*, because its compact foliage enables us to create an almost instant bonsai. With deciduous species you will have to build up the shape over two or three years.

Here are a few points to remember:

- Don't let the plant dictate the eventual size of the bonsai. Look for the 'tree within'.
- Where a trunk forks use the thinnest one as the leader to enhance trunk taper.
- Leave as many branches as possible to keep the tree vigorous; you can always prune them again in years to come.

1 *Clear all foliage and small shoots from the trunk, leaving the larger branches. Try to avoid leaving opposite branches.*

2 *Don't let the size of the original plant dictate the eventual size of the bonsai. Trim it judiciously.*

3 *The other leader is now shortened. This time a side shoot is left to become the new leader. Working this way, we are increasing trunk taper, making the tree appear older.*

4 *To start wiring the trunk, take a sturdy piece of wire and anchor it by pushing it into the soil close to the trunk.*

5 *Hold the trunk and wire together firmly and begin to coil. Hold close to the point where you are coiling and move your hand along the trunk.*

6 *Next wire the branches, using one piece of wire for two branches, as described on page 50. Wire right to the tip of each branch.*

7 *Grasp as much of the trunk as possible to spread the pressure and bend it into the desired shape.*

8 *Bend the branches down, making sure there are a few at the back. Bend close to the trunk. Clear any growth facing downwards.*

After a couple of hours our juniper already looks like a little tree. As time passes the trunk will thicken and the foliage pads will fill out. Low branches will be pruned and others allowed to extend as the shape is gradually developed and refined.

FIRST STEPS: SEEDLINGS

Nowadays most bonsai are created by reducing larger plants or by growing branches onto pre-formed trunks. However, there is still a very important place for growing bonsai straight from seed. It helps you to learn about the growth patterns of each species and makes you more aware of the structure of trees.

By growing bonsai from seed you can create an almost perfect little tree on a very small scale, without the need for heavy pruning. Being able to display a tiny, unblemished and well-formed bonsai that you grew from seed is a most satisfying and rewarding achievement.

Having pricked out your seedling as described on page 27, let it grow on unchecked for the rest of the season, since it is important to have an established root system before you begin training. The following year, during late spring/early summer, or as soon as the new growth has hardened off, you can make the first pruning cut. The purpose of this cut is to force the seedling to produce side branches, and it is the most drastic pruning you will ever need to do. Once the new branches have grown a little you can carry out the initial wiring as shown here.

You can plant your fledgling bonsai in a shallow but oversized container at the beginning of its third growing season. From now on, year after year, the continuing process of painstakingly wiring new shoots into position and regularly pinching out growing tips will gradually produce an incredibly realistic branch structure bearing a crop of tiny leaves.

1 *This typical hawthorn seedling is just beginning its third summer. It is pruned back to just three tiny spurs. Note the position and angle of the cut.*

- It is essential not to hurry the process. Remember that you are 'building' the final shape of the tree in much the same way as nature does. The longer you take to achieve the final shape the better the result will undoubtedly be.

- Try to plan the final size and shape of the bonsai in advance and pinch back to buds which will send the new growth in the desired direction.

2 *After three months the spurs have become strong shoots. Two will become branches and the third the new leader. Anchor the wire in the soil before coiling it around the trunk.*

3 *Now the trunk can be shaped. Bend from back to front as well as from side to side, avoiding exaggerated curves.*

- Never let run-away shoots grow out of control. They will thicken the parent branch out of proportion with the others and ruin the design. They will then have to be pruned and re-grown.

- Let new shoots put on three or four leaf nodes and then pinch back hard. If you try to grow each branch to its final intended length too soon it will not produce any forks.

Snipping off the apex encourages more branches to form.

4 *The branches have been wired, spread evenly and lowered to a horizontal position, and the trunk has a series of diminishing curves.*

5 *Shortening the stronger branches encourages new ones to form, as well as promoting side growth on the remaining ones.*

This eighteen-year-old hawthorn was grown in exactly the same way as demonstrated here. The bark was encouraged to crack and flake by wrapping it with loose, wet sphagnum moss for a year.

6 *Over the years the triangular shape will be allowed to become more rounded.*

Reducing Taller Trees

Some people prefer to grow very large bonsai but are unable to find suitable raw material growing in open ground, and are unwilling to spend the required number of years to grow their own. The only alternative is to acquire a suitable plant from a tree nursery.

1 *This twelve feet tall hornbeam* (Carpinus betulus) *was bought from a landscape tree nursery, and was chosen because it had plenty of low branches.*

Nursery trees are intended for planting in parks, streets or large gardens and are grown in the ground for a number of years before being established in containers prior to sale.

When seeking out such material make sure it is well established in its container. Examine the surface roots to ensure that they are evenly distributed. Scratch away a sliver of bark on each one – if it appears green beneath the bark the root is alive, if it appears brown or grey the root is dead.

Cutting off the top section of the trunk will force a tree to throw out shoots from the remaining trunk, but their location cannot be predicted and there is every chance that they will be limited to the area immediately around the cut. This is useless for bonsai purposes. So you will need to counter this by selecting a plant which has a good number of low branches.

The ideal time to carry out this initial pruning is in early spring, just before the buds break.

Leave the tree in its original container for at least a year before attempting to plant it in a bonsai pot. During this time you can begin to style it by wiring and pruning.

2 *Choose a branch for the new leader and make the cut diagonally downwards from this, towards a lower, opposite branch.*

3 *Use typewriter correction fluid to mark a natural flowing trunk line from the new leader to the top branch.*

5 *Seal the entire wound with cut paste* (see page 55), *making sure that the edges are well covered.*

4 *Carve the wound gradually up to the line without tearing the bark. Hollowing out the heartwood a little will help the wound to heal flat, resulting in an almost invisible scar.*

6 *The lower branches should now be kept trimmed to encourage fine twigs, while the top can grow freely for a year to help speed up the healing of the pruning scar.*

Left: *This hornbeam bonsai was created in exactly the same way as our demonstration. After four years the pruning scar has healed over and the leaves are reducing well.*

BONSAI TOOLS AND WIRE

All you really need in the way of equipment for your first attempts at growing bonsai are tools and a few other things which you probably already own.

TOOLS YOU WILL NEED

- A pair of sharp scissors
- Wire cutters
- Secateurs (bypass type, not anvil variety)
- Nail scissors for fine work
- A pointed steel hook for combing out roots.

These tools will do the job almost as well as the specialist Japanese bonsai tools shown here. But as you gain experience, you will begin to find them a little clumsy at best and totally inadequate at worst. Sooner or later you will want to invest in your first proper bonsai tools, but rather than spend a lot of money on a full set, buy them one or two at a time.

Because they are the cheapest tools, you will probably decide to buy a couple of pairs of scissors first, long ones for trimming and short shears for heavier work such as root pruning. This is a good choice and you will soon discover how easy the Japanese tools are to use.

Bottom left: *The range of wire that I find most useful. I only use the green, plastic-coated wire for anchoring the tree in its pot and for fashioning hooks and ties, etc. I get through a lot of wire, and it can be expensive if bought in small quantities. Once you know the thicknesses you use most, it is worth investing in some larger rolls.*

WIRE

On the opposite page we show a variety of types and thicknesses of wire. Your first choice may be influenced by economy and availability. Copper wire can be stripped from offcuts of electrical cable, and green, plastic-covered steel wire is readily available at garden centres.

However, once you have tried the custom-made product you will never want to use anything else. The wide variety of gauges and ease of manipulation make it a joy to work with, in spite of the extra expense.

Next you should go for some side cutters which can cut branches cleanly and accurately, and some long-handled wire cutters, designed to cut right up to the tip. The big advantages of both these tools is that they are able to reach the most inaccessible parts of the tree.

Curved branch cutters should come next. These are used for pruning close to the trunk, where a slight hollow is required to help the wound heal over quickly. Some bonsai pliers would be a good idea too. The shape of the jaws makes them ideal for stripping jins and sharis, as well as manipulating the wire once it has been applied to the tree. Acquire the other more specialist tools as and when necessary.

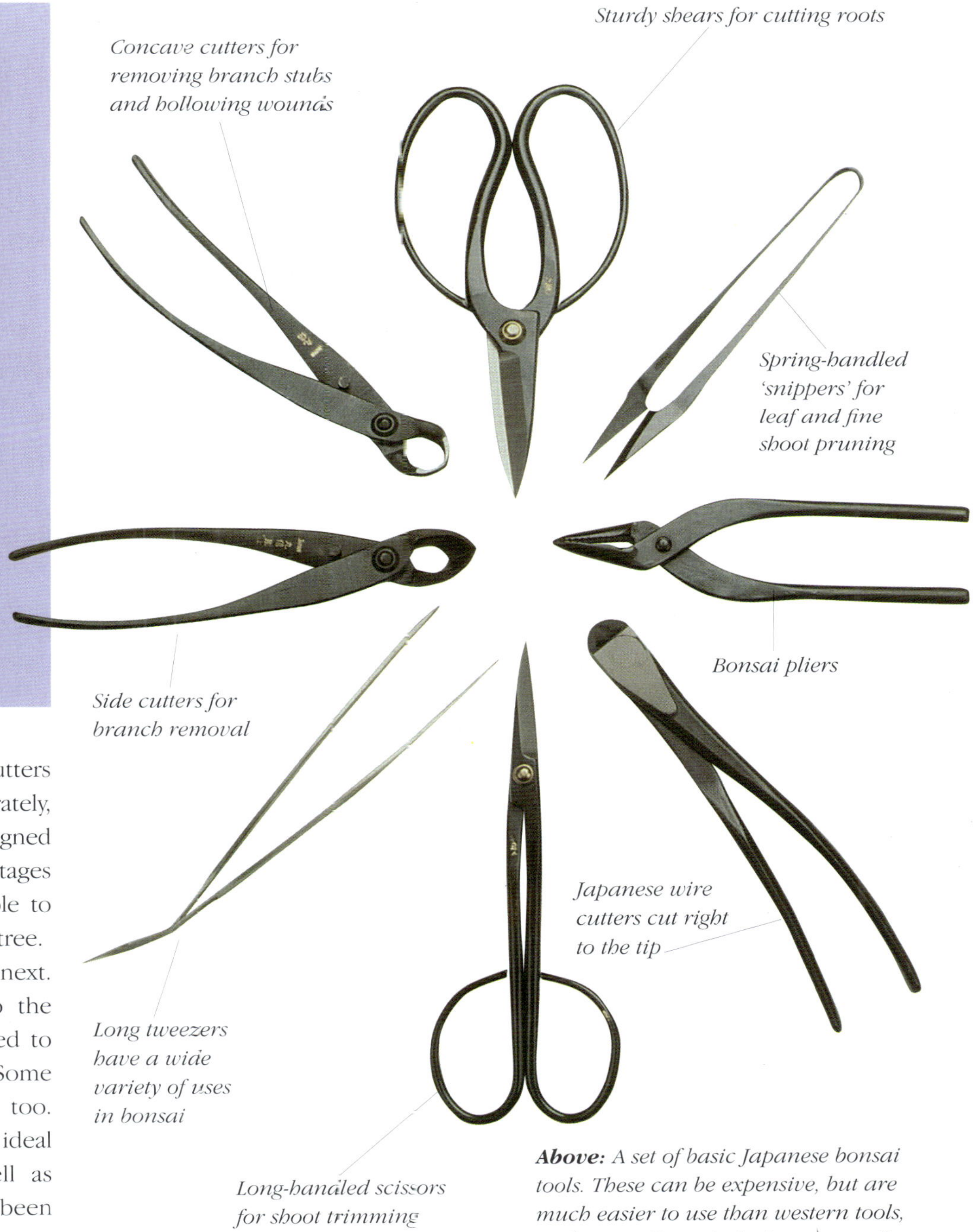

Above: *A set of basic Japanese bonsai tools. These can be expensive, but are much easier to use than western tools, and are well worth the investment if you intend to take the hobby seriously.*

SOILS

Most plants will survive for limited periods in almost any growing medium – clay, sand, even pure water – but in order to thrive they need rather more.

Since bonsai are grown in shallow containers for many years their requirements are quite specific. But before we discuss soil recipes let's consider the various functions of soil.

- The soil's most obvious function is to retain enough moisture and nutrients to ensure a steady supply to the roots between waterings.
- The soil must protect the roots from decay by allowing the free drainage of excess water.
- It must also contain air spaces so the roots can breathe.
- Finally, the soil anchors the tree in its pot, so it should not be too light.

SOIL RECIPES

The standard bonsai soil recipe, which has been tried and tested for many years, contains just two ingredients which, when sifted and mixed in roughly equal proportions, satisfy these four basic requirements.

NOTE: all soil ingredients must be well sifted to remove all the coarse lumps and, more importantly, all the fine particles.

ORGANIC MATTER

Organic matter satisfies the first of the four requirements mentioned above. This can be moss peat (as opposed to sedge peat), well-rotted leaf mould, composted forest bark or any of the peat substitutes which are becoming increasingly common.

Don't use any farmyard manure or garden compost, however well rotted, as you will risk introducing all manner of soil-borne diseases.

If you collect your own leaf mould, remove any unrotted material which will use up nitrogen from the fertiliser as it continues to decay. Also remove any insects or grubs that you may find.

GRIT

Grit, or sifted sharp sand, keeps the soil structure open and adds weight, thus satisfying the remaining three requirements.

Flint grit, as used for alpine composts, is good but it has sharp edges which can damage the roots if used carelessly. So be gentle when repotting and don't use too much pressure.

By far the best type I have tried is granite grit. The surface of each particle is uneven,

***Below:** More bonsai accessories: soil scoops, plastic mesh for covering drainage holes, a sturdy clamp for bending heavy branches, 'Kyonal' wound sealant and a rice haulm brush.*

but the edges are not sharp. Grit from fast-flowing streams is also good. Whatever kind of grit you use is not terribly important, however, so long as it is included.

ADDITIVES

Soil conditioners

An increasing number of soil conditioners are available to the amateur gardener, ranging from volcanic lava to calcined (baked) clay. The main advantage of using such additives is that they perform the same functions as both organic matter and grit. That is to say they drain well but also retain moisture. Some growers use calcined clay instead of organic matter, and others find trees grown in pure lava do exceptionally well. It is always worth experimenting.

Japanese Clay

Many bonsai nurseries now sell imported Japanese Akadama clay, which is specifically produced for bonsai. It retains its granular structure when wet, drains freely, retains moisture and air and allows the roots to grow through the particles. It sounds ideal, and indeed is in Japan, where the climate is predictable. But in our climate you may need to water your trees more often in summer, and keep them out of excessive rain during autumn and winter. However, it is worth trying.

Fertilisers

If you feed your bonsai properly it is not necessary to add fertiliser to the soil, but it does no harm to include a little bonemeal or fish, blood and bone. Add some trace element compound as a matter of course, since none of the ingredients can provide their own.

Crushed volcanic lava — *Japanese 'Akadama' cla.* — *Calcined (baked) clay*

Basic mix – 50:50 grit and peat — *Sifted peat, note the particle size* — *Flint grit (left) and crushed granite*

Above: *All bonsai enthusiasts have their own pet soil recipes, some better than others. The ingredients above have all been tried and tested over the years and have been found to be the best. You will see that loam, or garden soil has not been included. Garden soil not only contains all the soil-borne diseases, but it also quickly compacts when watered, forming a dense, soggy mass. Garden compost, farmyard manure and spent mushroom compost are also risky as they too can import many unwanted pests and diseases.*

VARIATIONS

PINES

Pines prefer a greater proportion of grit in the soil – up to eighty percent – and the tree's performance will be greatly enhanced if you can include pine needle mould in the mix. There is a naturally-occurring fungus associated with pines which covers the roots in a sheath known as a mycorrhiza. This breaks down the nutrients in the soil into a form which is more readily available to the tree in exchange for a share of the tree's manufactured food supply. It appears as fine white filaments called mycelium, which can be found just below the surface of pine litter.

FLOWERING AND FRUITING SPECIES

Producing flowers and fruit requires a great deal of energy, and any interruption to growth will sap the tree's strength and reduce its ability to perform for you. For this reason it is best to include extra organic matter or clay, to increase the reservoir for nutrients, and to use a fairly deep pot.

Pots

A bonsai pot is more than just a container for the plant to grow in. It is an integral part of the composition and must complement the tree to form a harmonious unit. Here we show you a selection of different types of pot and indicate what styles or species they best suit.

As well as aesthetic considerations, the pot also has to satisfy some practical requirements, so the following points should be remembered when buying pots:

- Ensure the pot is stoneware, which is frost-proof, as opposed to earthenware, which is not. Earthenware pots will rapidly disintegrate with the first hard frost. A simple test is to wet the unglazed surface of the pot to see if it absorbs the water. If it does it is earthenware, if the water wipes off cleanly the pot is stoneware.
- There must be excellent drainage. The holes should be at least three times greater in number and size than in a conventional flower pot.
- The floor of the pot must be level, so that no pockets of water can accumulate in the base. Check that there are no indentations in the corners where the feet are fixed.
- All pots must have feet in order to leave space for the drained water to flow away.
- Avoid pots which are glazed on the inside. This provides an inhospitable surface for the roots and will cause the soil to dry out too quickly around the perimeter of the pot.

A number of nurseries now sell pots made of mica, which retail at less than half the price of stoneware pots. These look authentic, but the surface scratches easily, so they are unsuitable for exhibiting.

Opposite: *There is a wide selection of full-sized bonsai pots now available to the bonsai enthusiast.*

Below: *Mame pots, although only tiny, are similar in shape and quality to the full sized ones, although they tend to be more colourful. The art of the mame potter is so appreciated by some enthusiasts that they become collectors' items in their own right, even though they may never be used.*

Left: *This shallow, elegant, round pot in a gentle unglased grey, would suit 'feminine' styles such as literati, or thin-trunked deciduous clumps.*

Below: *Strong, flared, unglazed rectangle, suitable for heavy-trunked conifers, especially driftwood styles.*

Right: *Sturdy, cream-glazed ovals like this look good with maples and elms. They are too delicate for strong conifer images.*

Above right: *The subtle grey-green glaze on this elegant rectangle would suit most broadleaved species and styles, and could look good with informal, upright larches, too.*

Above: *Standard brown, unglazed Kobi-ware rectangle. If in doubt, this type of pot will do for almost anything.*

Above: *Very shallow oval glazed pot, designed specifically with group plantings in mind.*

Left: *This 'drum' style pot is made in a variety of sizes and is best used for strong-trunked literati or formal upright styles. It could also be successfully used for heavy clumps.*

REPOTTING AND ROOT PRUNING

The thought of root pruning fills most bonsai novices with horror, but it is essential in order to maintain the tree's health and vigour. If the process is ignored your bonsai will become pot bound. It will weaken, shed shoots and branches and eventually die.

WHY PRUNE THE ROOTS?

In the wild a tree will extend its roots each growing season in much the same way as it produces new shoots. These new roots do most of the work, absorbing water and nutrients. As the tree matures some older roots will die back, only to be replaced by strong, new ones.

However, things are different in a pot. You have to reproduce this cycle artificially in order to keep your bonsai healthy. Health means vigour, and a vigorous tree is more able to resist disease and can outgrow attacks by pests. It will also respond better to training techniques.

A healthy young bonsai – say up to ten years old – in a small pot will pack its container with roots within one season, so it will need to be root pruned each year. Older trees, especially conifers, tend to grow more slowly, taking perhaps up to five years to fill the pot. However, before you start to panic, remember that it takes time for problems associated with root confinement to take effect, and you can miss a year every so often without putting your tree at risk.

1 *After two years, the roots of this medium-size trident maple are filling the pot, and need to be pruned. They are all healthy, and as you can see, they have already started to grow. The fine, white vertical roots are from winter weed seeds.*

2 *Lift the tree from its pot and carefully comb out the roots. Work from the centre outwards. Use a chopstick, knitting needle, or whatever else comes to hand.*

3 *Comb out the underneath of the root mass as well, without tearing them. When you have finished you should have removed about a third of the total volume of soil.*

4 *Trim the roots back so that the remaining root mass doesn't quite fill the pot. Use a good, sharp pair of scissors, but mind the grit.*

5 *It is important to trim the roots underneath as well, otherwise the tree will rise in its pot as it grows. Thick roots should be pruned hard back to encourage compact growth.*

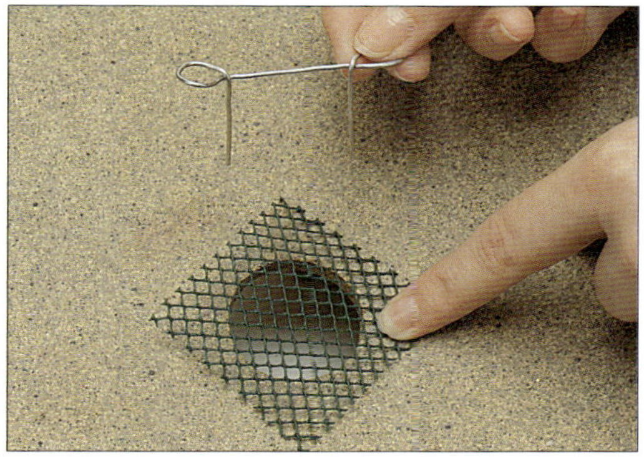

6 *You can repot the tree in the same container or in a more suitable one as we are doing. First, cover the drainage holes with mesh, held in place with wire loops like these.*

7 *Push the wire through the mesh and drainage holes and bend the 'legs' up tight against the underneath of the pot.*

8 *Some pots have additional small holes for tie wires. If not, you can use the drainage holes. You need at least two pieces of wire to make the tree secure until the roots have re-established.*

9 *Cover the floor of the pot with coarse grit to aid drainage. If the pot is less than an inch deep you do not need a drainage course, provided the soil is sufficiently free-draining.*

10 *Cover the grit with a layer of fresh soil. This must be well sifted to remove all the fine particles. Make a small mound of soil where the trunk will sit.*

1 *Nestle the tree into the mound of soil, placing it just off-centre, for best aesthetic effect, with the surface of the root mass just below the pot's rim.*

2 *Next pull the wire ties down over the root mass and twist them together until the tree does not rock. Cushion the bark with squares of rubber or foam.*

WHEN TO ROOT PRUNE

The ideal time for root pruning is just as the roots begin to grow in spring. The exact timing depends on the advancement of the season, geographical location and the species. Deciduous trees, particularly trident maples and elms, start producing new roots as early as mid-February in the south of England but not until a month later in the north. Pines may not start new root growth in earnest until April in the south and as late as May further north.

EMERGENCY REPOTTING

Sometimes it is necessary to repot a tree 'out of season'. An emergency is likely when you inspect the roots of an ailing tree and notice they are decaying, or worse still, missing! This may be due to fungal attack, most likely resulting from poor drainage or over feeding, or to the appetite of a subterranean pest. In either instance, take the following action:

- Defoliate all deciduous trees to reduce water loss. Do not defoliate evergreens.
- Very gently comb away all the dead roots and soil. Then, equally gently, hose away all the remaining soil. Inspect what is left thoroughly, remove any larvae and remaining dead roots. Don't cut any living roots if you can help it.
- Plant the tree in an oversized container, using a soil mix of at least eighty percent grit and no loam. Bury the roots deeper than before and water, using a solution of systemic fungicide.
- Place the tree in either a humid, but ventilated poly-tunnel, or home-made polythene tent, and spray at least once a day.
- Maintain an evenly damp soil. There should be just enough moisture to satisfy the tree's reduced needs but little enough to encourage the roots to grow in search of more.

The first sign of root activity is a slight swelling of the buds on last year's shoots. Gently lift the tree from its pot and take a close look at the roots. If the tips appear to be swelling, the time is right. If the tips are white they have already started to grow, but pruning will do them no harm so long as the new buds have not opened yet.

If, on the other hand, your tree is due for repotting in theory and the buds have begun to swell but the visible roots appear brown and dead, this may be an indication of decay. You should therefore repot immediately. *(See 'Emergency Repotting', opposite.)*

It is a good idea to inspect the roots of all your bonsai periodically, whether they are due for root pruning or not. This is particularly important if the tree is looking a bit off colour. As often as not, lack of vigour, wilting or premature leaf-fall is a symptom of a root-related problem such as decay or attack by the voracious vine weevil larva (see page 90).

After repotting, wait two weeks before commencing heavy pruning, and delay feeding for four to six weeks, or until new growth has been established.

This is an ideal time to do the odd bit of wiring

Our newly-repotted tree now needs to be placed in a sheltered position until new growth starts. It should not be watered again until really necessary, and not fed for four weeks, to avoid burning the tender new roots.

Note how last year's shoots have been pruned to an outward-facing bud

3 *Fill the remaining spaces with fresh soil. If the soil is virtually dry it is a lot easier to apply, because it runs freely and does not compact.*

4 *Work the soil in between the roots, ensuring that there are no air pockets. Use either your fingers or a chopstick, in the traditional way.*

5 *Water the newly potted tree well, but use a fine rose or spray, so you don't wash away the new soil.*

SHAPING WITH WIRE

Wiring is the most fundamental process in bonsai training, allowing the accurate positioning of branches and shoots. The principle is simple but the skill does take a little time to acquire.

Wire of a suitable gauge is coiled around a branch or shoot. The two can then be bent and manoeuvred into the desired position, and the wire will hold the branch in place. After a period of growth has taken place, the branch will set in that position and the wire can be removed (see page 52).

The time taken for this to happen varies from one species to another. Conifers, especially junipers, may take several years to set, during which time the wire may need to be removed and reapplied several times to avoid damaging the bark. Some deciduous species may set in a matter of a few weeks.

Older, stiffer branches will also take longer, and you may have to bend them little by little every few weeks until the desired position is achieved. Every plant is an individual, and it is only with experience that you will learn just how far you can go before snapping the branch, so take it easy at first.

Before you embark on your first wiring exercise, you should practise the technique on a twig or branch from a garden shrub – preferably a species similar to the one you have chosen for your bonsai. See how thick the wire needs to be, and how far the branch will bend without breaking.

The branches on this old 'shimpaku' juniper from Japan would have been wired into position many years ago, while they were young and flexible.

WHAT WIRE?

Custom made aluminium wire is readily available from all bonsai outlets and by mail order. This is anodised to give it an unobtrusive brown finish, and although it is suitable for most purposes it can be expensive. Silver wire may also be used.

The Japanese traditionally use copper wire for conifers because its superior holding power is more effective on their springier branches. If aluminium wire is used, it needs to be much thicker and is therefore more unsightly.

1 *For your first try, use fairly thick wire which is easier to handle. Always hold the wired part of the branch firmly with one hand and coil the wire with the other.*

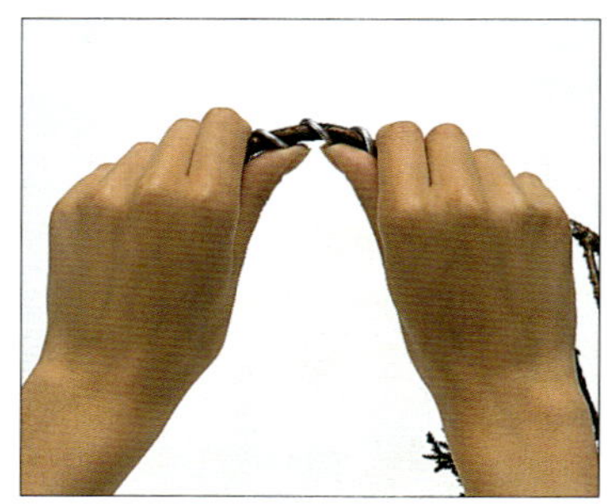

2 *When you bend the branch, do it gradually. Spread your hands so you hold as much of the branch as possible and use both thumbs as leverage points.*

3 *Once bent, the wire should hold the branch in position. If the branch springs back, the wire is too thin, if it cuts the bark, it is too tight.*

4 *When wiring long branches, reduce the thickness of the wire as the branch diameter decreases. Overlap the different thicknesses by two or three turns.*

CORRECT WIRING

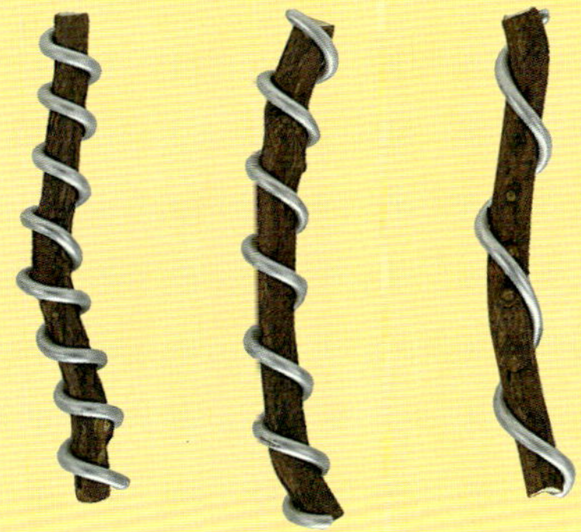

The example on the left shows the coils too close together. This reduces the holding power and restricts the sap flow. On the right, the coils are too far apart and would have very little holding power. The example in the centre shows ideal wiring. The coils are at approximately 45 degrees.

7 *It is also best to use one piece of wire for forked branches. Make sure you coil it in opposite directions in each branch, otherwise the wire on the first branch will uncoil as you work on the second one.*

6 *The best plan is to use one piece of wire for two branches, which provides perfect anchorage. Coil the wire in the directions shown here.*

5 *When wiring a side branch, anchor the wire by coiling it around the trunk. Always take it through the fork of the branch as shown.*

Plastic-coated iron wire is sold in two thicknesses in garden centres and can be used as a last resort, but is too stiff and consequently more difficult to apply safely.

HOW THICK?

With a little experience you will soon be able to assess what gauge of wire will be needed for any given branch. Remember that doubling the thickness of your wire for heavier branches will increase the holding power by a factor of three.

HOW MUCH?

Plan your wiring 'strategy' in advance. Decide where you want the wiring to begin and end, and cut a piece at least a third longer than the length of the branch. If you are going to use twin wires, use one piece doubled up. Start by anchoring the end where the pieces are joined and work them both together along the branch.

CLAMPS

Sometimes you may want to create a sharp bend, or alter the direction of a really thick branch or trunk, where no amount of wire would have any effect. In such cases special clamps can be employed. They are available in several sizes, the largest one being capable of bending a conifer branch over one inch thick.

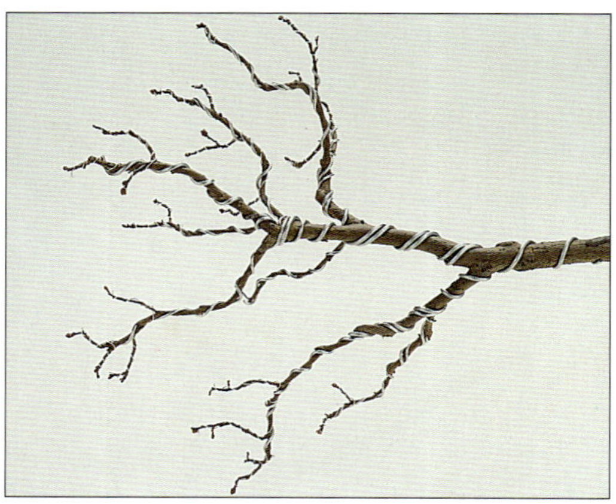

1 *A plan view of a fully wired deciduous branch. Note how the side branches are fanned out like spread fingers, and how straight lines are avoided.*

2 *Side view of the same branch. It is important to build height on the branches of deciduous trees, as well as width, in order to promote the best possible form for the tree as a whole. There is plenty of space left between each shoot for future growth to come through.*

3 *Pine branches are wired to a different shape. The side branches should cascade slightly from the main limb, forming a low dome. The tip of each shoot is wired to point upwards.*

4 *A plan view of a juniper branch, shaped in the traditional way for the formal upright style. Note the triangular shape and how the side branches are positioned alternately. On junipers and pines, stripping old foliage like this allows light to stimulate back budding. For some curious reason, the wire itself also seems to have a similar effect.*

REMOVING WIRE

Wire can be expensive, so it is tempting to unwind it once it has served its purpose, in order to use it another time. However this is a risky business, since it is much easier to damage the bark, or even snap the branch, when working in reverse. The branch will have swollen so the wire will be tighter than when you first applied it, and will naturally be full of kinks, making it difficult to manipulate.

It is much safer to snip the wire away using wire cutters which cut right up to the tip of the jaws. Custom-made Japanese bonsai wire cutters are designed for this purpose, but can be quite expensive. To start with, good quality electrical wire cutters will do the job just as well if you choose the tool carefully. You will need the long-handled type to enable you to reach awkward places. Any damage to the bark caused by the cutters will be superficial and will heal much quicker than damaged caused through careless uncoiling. If you are worried about the unnecessary expense of 'wasting' wire in this way, ask yourself this question: what is the most valuable to you, a few inches of wire or a developing bonsai which you have laboured over for hours and nurtured for years?

5 *If the wire stays on too long it will cut right into the bark like this. Remove it in good time and, if the branch hasn't set, rewire it, coiling in the opposite direction.*

BRANCH PRUNING

When a branch is pruned it will inevitably leave a scar. With full-sized trees the wound will normally heal rapidly and any resulting disfiguration will be of little or no consequence. However, since bonsai grow more slowly the healing process is slower as well, so it needs all the help it can get.

When pruning branches, great care must be taken to minimise the possibility of unsightly swellings around the wound, and to encourage the scar to blend in with the character of the trunk.

Here we show you how to execute simple pruning, where a small to medium sized branch is removed. We also show how to use a larger wound to your advantage, by hollowing it out and turning it into an interesting feature. Here are a few general points to bear in mind:

- Always use very sharp tools, which should ideally be sterilised in methylated spirit.
- The cambium layer (between the bark and the heartwood) must be sealed against frost, water and drying wind. If left exposed it may die back.
- Never use bitumen-based sealants. These will dry hard and will be impossible to remove without causing disfiguration.
- Feed the tree well after drastic pruning to speed up the healing process.
- Any unwanted shoots which arise from around the wound must be rubbed off thoroughly as soon as they appear. Failure to do this will result in disfiguration and lots of ugly swellings around the tree's scar.

Below: *Avoid pruning a branch in the front of the trunk, as here. The scar will be in the most noticeable place of all.*

1 *If you don't have any bonsai tools, some sharp secateurs will do. Use the 'bypass' type rather than the 'anvil' type.*

2 *Leave a small stub at first, rather than cutting right up to the trunk. You will damage the bark on the trunk if you are impatient.*

DISGUISING LARGE WOUNDS

Sometimes it is necessary to prune away really heavy branches, causing scars which would normally take many years to heal. Even then, they might be too large to be in proportion with the rest of the bonsai.

You can turn these large scars to your advantage by hollowing out the wound, right through to the heartwood. If carried out with care this can result in a natural looking feature which will add age and character to the trunk.

You need to use very sharp gouges or routers when carving into bonsai trees.

This hollow trunk has acquired all the character of an ancient, full-sized tree.

3 *Finish off the cut as close to the trunk as possible. It will heal more neatly if you create a slight hollow in the exposed wood.*

4 *Clean up the edges of the wound with a sharp knife. This will deter fungal spores which may later infect the whole tree.*

5 *Seal the wound thoroughly, especially at the edges, with special bonsai sealant or wax and oil.*

MAINTENANCE PRUNING

Each year your bonsai will throw out new shoots from the buds created in the leaf axils during the previous growing season. It will only take a few weeks for these shoots to outgrow the design of the tree and make it look very scruffy.

It takes many hours each winter to carry out maintenance pruning on this trident maple in order to keep the fine twig structure.

In a developing or semi-mature bonsai these shoots can be allowed to grow to six or seven leaves before they are cut back. Allowing them this period of free growth thickens the parent branches and trunk and builds up a general vigour in the tree. If allowed to grow too long they will sap the strength from the finer growth and will quickly kill it off. New shoots will emerge from the buds in the remaining leaf axils. Any wayward shoots, or those which are destined to become new branches, should be wired at this stage.

However, in established bonsai this annual growth will need to be cut back during the dormant season to allow the next season's growth room to extend before outgrowing the design. Over the seasons this constant 'clip-and-grow' technique will reward you with a much-forked branch structure, with all the characteristics of an ancient tree.

Here we show how to approach the winter pruning of trees with alternate and opposite leaves – in this case English elm and Japanese maple. Always remember to prune to a bud which points in the direction you want the new growth to take. It is possible to style a bonsai

1 *During the previous growing season this maple produced a few long shoots. The first step is to cut them back to a short shoot, or spur.*

2 *Every few years it is necessary to prune away older growth to prevent overcrowding and to maintain neat foliage pads.*

3 *Finally, cut back all spurs to one or two buds. You may have to look quite closely to see the buds because they can be minute. Look carefully at the base of each spur.*

4 *After a good prune the branch looks rather naked, but remember that every remaining bud will generate a new shoot next season, producing an ever-more-compact twig structure.*

5 *Like the maple, this elm has grown some long shoots which need to be pruned first in order for the tree to look neat and tidy.*

6 *Unwanted shoots arising from older wood should also be cut off. Notice the edges of bud development. This is an ideal time for maintenance pruning, since you can easily see where all the minute buds are located.*

7 *This is also a good time to prune off any dead shoots. Each shoot has been pruned to a bud facing in the direction the new growth is required.*

8 *Each of the remaining shortened shoots bears dormant buds around its base, which will sprout in the future, thus ensuring a never ending supply of new shoots.*

SUMMER PINCHING

Summer pinching involves several carefully refined techniques to ensure that the new growth that appears each growing season does not starve the inner structure of the tree. It is essential for the continued smooth development of almost any bonsai.

Once the branch structure has become established there should be enough new shoots appearing each spring, bearing sufficient foliage to sustain the tree without necessarily allowing any extension growth. Extension growth draws the energy from the rest of the tree, concentrating it in the growing tips. This starves the fine inner twigs of nutrients and the additional foliage prevents them gaining adequate light. The result is that the fine twigs die and the whole twig development process will need to be started all over again.

First we have to build and refine this tracery of fine twigs. Once this has been done the resulting foliage pads must be kept trimmed and in balance with the design. Both these ends are achieved by pinching out the tips of all new growth as it appears.

Different species grow in different ways, and the following techniques have been developed to accommodate the five most common growth patterns.

With broadleaved trees new shoots will emerge from the buds in the remaining leaf axils.

In pines new buds will form at the point at which the shoot is pinched, as well as further back on older growth.

SPECIAL POINTS

- Larch and spruce will only produce new shoots from buds which are already visible on the remaining shoot or from around the base of the shoot and on older growth.
- Junipers will throw out new growth from any branch or shoot which bears foliage, and need constant pinching throughout the growing season.

1 *Spruce buds open to form tiny, bright green tufts which should be plucked before they have fully elongated. Don't do the whole tree at one go: spread the job over two weeks.*

2 As pine buds begin to grow they elongate, forming 'candles' which should have up to two thirds snapped off before the needles develop.

3 Junipers produce prolific new growth, forming tightly-packed foliage. This extension growth is distinguished by its lighter colour. Hold the fan of foliage in one hand and pull out all extending growth with the finger and thumb of the other.

4 Zelkovas and other alternate-leaved species produce new leaves one at a time at the shoot tips. This leaf, and the minute bud at its base, should be pinched out, using tweezers if necessary.

This magnificent Japanese maple is grown in the unusual split-trunk style. The delicately-coloured spring foliage adopts a pose like that of trees seen in Japanese prints.

5 Maples produce new leaves in pairs borne on a short extending shoot. Both leaves should be carefully pinched out, together with the tiny developing bud nestled between them.

LEAF PRUNING

This is the ultimate refinement technique which is only suitable for broadleaved deciduous species. It results in a very fine, compact twig formation, tiny leaves and enhanced autumn colour in the year it is applied.

1 *This shohin field maple received a merit award from Saburo Kato, president of the World Bonsai Federation. Being small, it needs regular leaf pruning to reduce the scale of the leaves.*

Leaf pruning can also be employed as a device for reducing transpiration after emergency out-of-season repotting *(see page 48)*.

Since this technique causes a certain amount of stress to the tree it should only be carried out every three years or so, and only on trees which are in good health and vigour. For this reason its use is normally restricted to bonsai which are in preparation for exhibition. The ideal time for leaf pruning is early summer, as soon as the spring growth has hardened.

The principle is similar to shoot pruning and pinching, in that the reduction of foliage encourages new side growth to take place. But because the foliage is totally removed the tree undergoes a 'false autumn' and next year's growth develops this year. This means that there will be a much greater number of new shoots than existed before, bearing correspondingly more leaves.

Since the tree can only support – and only requires – a fixed volume of foliage, these leaves will be greatly reduced in size. Also, since these leaves only have half a season to live, they will be in better condition come autumn, resulting in brighter colour over a longer period.

2 *Even though it may seem a little unnerving at first, take the plunge and start snipping off all the leaves, one by one.*

3 *Cut just below the leaf, leaving the petiole, or leaf stalk, intact. Making the cut in this manner will prevent excessive 'bleeding' from the leaf stalk and is kinder to the tree as a whole. Provided the tree is vigorous and healthy, radical pruning of foliage should not create problems, so long as it is conducted in a sensitive manner and not carried out too often. Don't worry too much about harming your tree.*

4 *Leaf pruning also presents an ideal opportunity to check the progress of the branch structure The petioles which remain on the tree will fall as soon as the new leaves start to emerge.*

5 *After a week or two the new crop of leaves emerges, brighter and even more colourful than in the first flush of spring.*

6 *Less than a month later the tree has grown a full crop of small, brightly-coloured leaves, borne on short shoots. Suddenly what seemed like drastic surgery makes good sense, as the tree is renewed almost beyond recognition!*

THE PROJECTS

BROOM STYLE ZELKOVA

There is only one species which is eminently suitable for this style – the Japanese grey-barked elm, *zelkova serrata*, and it is no coincidence that it grows in this habit in nature. Other deciduous species can be used, but none perform as well.

The creation of such a geometric, uniform branch structure requires an equally precise and calculated approach, which is usually successful. The only element of chance is in the placement of the new shoots as they emerge from the severed trunk. However, there are normally so many that you would be very unlucky not to get off to a good start.

1 *Before you start, make sure the plant is in good health and is firmly tied into its container. This will help prevent too much strain on the roots during cutting. The best time for this technique is early spring, before the production of new foliage has used up any of the tree's stored energy.*

2 *Decide how tall you want the trunk to be – the ideal proportion is about four times its width. Using a very sharp, fine-toothed saw, make two cuts which form an unequal sided, 'V'-shaped surface.*

3 *Clean up any ragged edges with a sharp knife and seal the entire cut surface, especially around the edge, where the cambium layer is located.*

The plant you select must have a trunk thickness anything from three-quarters of an inch to four inches or more. Once the sequence illustrated has been followed, adopt an annual regime of allowing shoots to grow four or five leaves and then trimming back to two. A vigorous, well fed tree may require this treatment several times during each growing season. Gradually you will build up a network of evenly spaced branches with ever-decreasing internodes.

4 *When shoots emerge, tie some waterproof tape tightly around them. This ensures a smooth transition from trunk to branch without swelling.*

6 *New shoots will grow from each leaf axil, and they, too, will be shortened. This cycle will need to be repeated many times over.*

Below: *A classic broom style, or* hokidachi, *zelkova. It would have taken up to ten years or more to develop this fine tracery of twigs.*

5 *The new shoots will grow rapidly. By the time they have reached this size they will have hardened off and will be ready for a prune.*

Regular pruning over many years is responsible for this uniform branch structure

The pattern of the branches is reflected in the surface root formation

INFORMAL UPRIGHT MAPLE

Once a young tree has been allowed to thicken to about half an inch or so it becomes virtually impossible to bend. However, you can still take advantage of the tree's natural resilience to create an informal upright style with severe taper, by employing this 'prune-and-grow' technique.

Any deciduous species can be used but Japanese maples are the best. The fact that they have opposite leaves, and therefore produce new shoots opposite each other, creates a mechanical growth pattern. This enables you to position the branches exactly on the outside of bends in the trunk and also means that the branch structure will echo the trunk's angular form.

The tree featured here has retained two small, weak branches which mark the position of the end of the first season's growth. These will be developed to become the new leader and the first major branch.

If these branches are not present you will still be able to detect the 'eyes' of the dormant buds from which such branches will grow. The initial cut should be made precisely as shown, and within a few weeks the new shoots will emerge. This operation should be carried out in early spring.

This process of allowing extension growth and pruning back to suitable positioned shoots or nodes should be repeated another two to four times – no more – before the final height is attained. A tree with too many sharp bends in a tall trunk looks unnatural.

1 *The roots of this newly-dug Japanese maple are wrapped to preserve moisture while the trunk is cut directly above the bottom two branches or dormant buds.*

2 *The branch on the left is chosen to become the new leader and is pruned at the point where the next angle is planned, just above a pair of buds. The large wound must be sealed.*

3 *Select a large clay pot to encourage rapid growth. The long roots should be shortened to promote a compact root structure.*

4 *Plant the tree at an angle so that one branch is horizontal, and the other – the new leader – points upwards at a similar angle to the trunk, but in the opposite direction.*

5 *Maples produce a lot of small shoots around pruning scars. These should be thinned out so all the tree's energy is concentrated in the developing trunk.*

6 *Two shoots are left to become the second branch and the new leader. This time another shoot is also left at the rear to form the first back branch.*

7 *Another few weeks pass and the maple is ready for its third prune of the season. Free draining soil with frequent watering and feeding produces this vigorous growth, essential for rapid trunk development.*

8 *The third pruning leaves three side branches, one to the rear, and four sections of trunk. One more year and the structure will be complete.*

BEECH GROUP

Most species can be used for creating bonsai groups and the results can be almost instantly satisfying. The main effect is achieved by the interplay between the trunks of different thicknesses and lines, and the actual branch structure is less important than it is with a single tree.

Successful groups can be created from young, spindly plants which would normally be little or no use as single trees, so this is a good way to utilise seedlings or cuttings which you would otherwise discard.

We have chosen some rooted beech cuttings which were intended for hedging.

1 *These beech cuttings are not particularly inspiring at first sight, but their different thicknesses and lines are just what we need to create a group.*

This type of raw material is usually sold in large numbers, so it is very cheap, and there is always plenty to choose from. Other hedging stock includes hawthorn, elm, privet, field maple and so on.

It is important to select plants of different heights and thicknesses in order to create perspective and interest. Stick to odd numbers, they are easier to compose (the Japanese actually have a superstitious aversion to even numbers), and avoid the temptation to use too many plants at first. A group of more than nine or so becomes a forest, which is subject to slightly different aesthetic principles.

Create your group in early spring, and keep it in a humid and well ventilated place, such as an open-ended polytunnel, until the roots are established and growth is evident. Little or no wiring should be necessary since the foliage will hide the branches and will merely act as a visual foil to the trunk arrangement. Any branches growing towards the centre of the group should be removed and from then on all you will need to do is prune new growth and thin out cluttered shoots.

2 *Cut away the long roots with sharp scissors, leaving as many fine feeder roots as possible on what remains of the rootball.*

3 *Work a sticky mixture of equal parts of clay and fine peat between the roots, and mould them into a ball.*

4 *The clay balls keep the trees in position while they are being arranged in the pot. Start with the tallest tree, just off centre, and place the two next tallest either side.*

5 *Build up the design tree by tree, adding the smaller ones at the sides and rear to create perspective. Leaning the trees away from the centre gives the illusion of greater size.*

6 *When the arrangement is complete, carefully add soil between the clay balls. Dry soil is easier to apply as it does not stick to the wet clay.*

Below: *You can complete the picture by 'landscaping' the soil surface with different kinds of moss and grit. Water the pot and moss thoroughly first, and avoid pressing the moss down too hard. The new planting is now already pleasing to the eye. Note how the trees at the edges have been pruned so each apex sweeps outwards.*

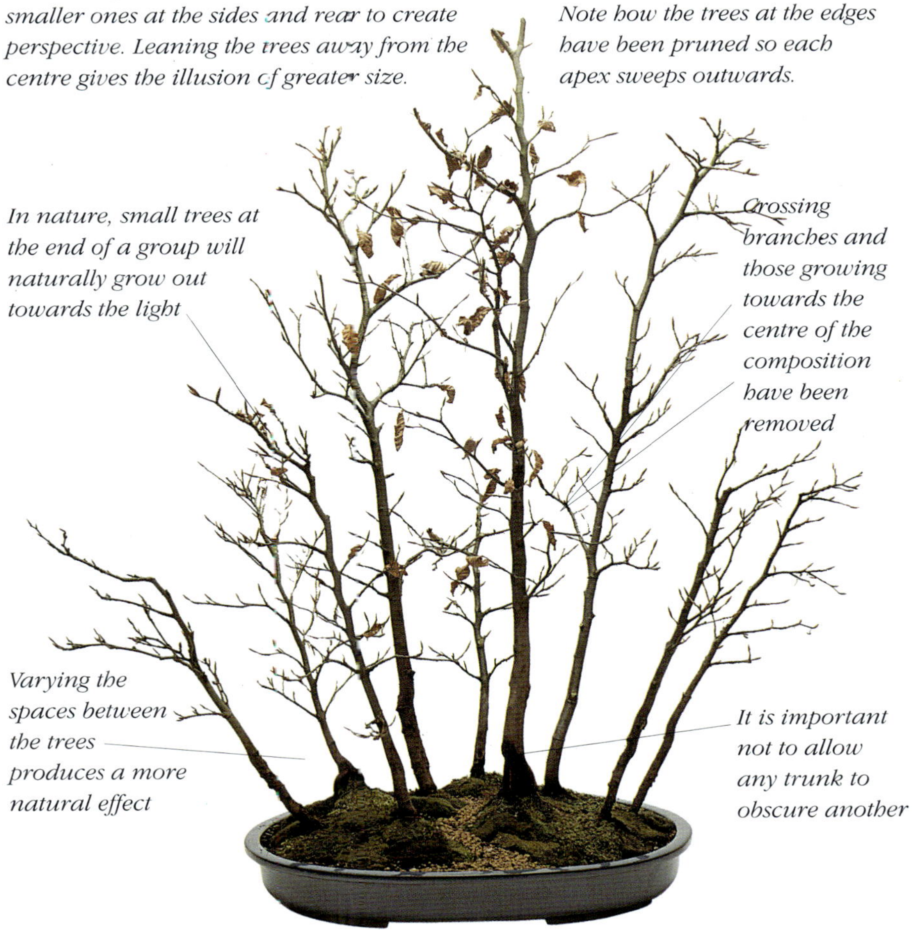

FOREST ON A SLAB

Most species capable of producing relatively tall, slender trunks can be used for forest plantings. However, the most important thing to remember when planting a forest is that it should have depth and perspective as well as width.

For all forest plantings, avoid trees which produce a proliferation of back buds, such as cotoneaster or Chinese elm. These will soon become congested and will be a nightmare to keep thinned out. Pines are also seldom used in large numbers, since they are prone to disease when overcrowded, but most other conifers are eminently suitable.

Although the actual front-to-back depth of the pot – or more often slab – may be only a foot or so, the objective is to create the illusion of several hundred yards at least and hint at an almost infinite unseen depth.

FOREST PLANTING TIPS

- Select plants of different heights and thicknesses.
- For width, plant the largest trees towards the centre and front and reduce the heights progressively at either side and behind.
- For perspective, plant the smallest trees at the back.
- A few smaller trees planted in front will look younger rather than further away.
- No three trees should be in a straight line when viewed from *any* angle.
- When viewed from the front, no trunk should be obscured by another. Allow the eye unimpeded access to the whole forest.

1 *The first step is to choose your stone slab, which should ideally have an irregular, narrow shape. This one is about three feet long.*

2 *Build a low wall with a sticky mix of clay and fine peat to stop the soil washing off the slab. Leave a generous margin of at least a couple of inches around the wall and fill the inside with a one-inch thick layer of soil.*

3 *Choose young plants of different sizes. Forest trees have tall, clean trunks, so you will need to trim off all the lower branches.*

4 *Start by placing the tallest tree towards one end of the slab and near the front. Add a slightly smaller tree either side and a little further back.*

5 *Repeat at the other end of the slab. Now arrange the smaller trees around these two clumps.*

6 *Carefully work dry soil between all the roots and gently firm it down.*

Right: *This newly created forest already has a realistic appearance. As with smaller groups, care must be taken to avoid overlapping the trunks and to vary the spaces between them.*

RAFT PLANTING

There is an old saying that has a particular relevance to bonsai forest plantings which neatly summarises the whole point of creating them: *'Plant a tree and let it grow. Let that tree set seed and after five hundred years you may have a forest.'*

1 *Blaauws junipers* (juniperus media blaauwii) *like this are common in all garden centres, and are quite inexpensive.*

2 *Lay the plant on its side and wire-train all the branches upwards. Try to spread them to give a three-dimensional effect, and bring the lower branches back towards the roots.*

Of course in bonsai there are much quicker and more efficient ways to create realistic forests in miniature, and the raft technique is the most reliable of all.

The raft technique has one major advantage over the traditional method of using individual trees of different ages. This is simply that each 'tree' doesn't have to compete with its neighbours for food and water, so there is little risk of the smaller and weaker ones dying off. It also means that each individual 'tree' is identical in colour and vigour.

The process is simple and can be successfully applied to any species. All you need is a plant with as many branches as possible of different thicknesses and lengths all tending to grow from one side of the trunk. It will help with the design if the plant also has some very low branches as you will see.

With Blaauws juniper you can carry out this operation at any time between February and June, but with other species early spring is best. After a year or two the new roots will be able to support the tree on their own and the original root mass can be cut off.

3 *Cut out some sections of bark on the underside of the trunk. New roots will form around the wounds, which will sustain the tree when the original roots are eventually removed.*

4 *Carefully comb out the roots, especially on the underside of the root ball, taking care not to cause unnecessary damage. Any heavy roots which grow upwards can be cut off.*

5 *Gently fold the roots underneath the trunk and lay the whole thing flat on a one-inch bed of bonsai soil in a suitable shallow container. Spread the roots out over the soil.*

6 *New roots will not form along the trunk unless it is covered with soil. Wire through the drainage holes will hold the trunk down firmly.*

This raft style needle juniper is very old, and has developed into a classic bonsai. The tallest trunk is nearly three feet high.

You can still see the original trunk just below the soil surface

Note how the trunks fan out from the base

7 *Mound more soil over the trunk and roots. Work it between the branches.*

8 *Moss and grit can be added to create a realistic effect. Once the new planting has grown a little, the trunks and branches can be properly wire-trained.*

SHOHIN, EXPOSED ROOT STYLE

Dwarf spruce (*Picea* 'little gem') is very easy to work with. The growth is so profuse and compact that you can style the basic bonsai shape with very little wiring.

Spruce tolerates root pruning well and readily produces back budding. It is a perfect species for creating *shohin* or miniature bonsai. (The phrase 'shohin' literally translates as 'small goods'). There is no official size restriction for shohin but they are generally no taller than six or seven inches. The Japanese say 'feel' is more important than size.

Shohin bonsai need more careful watering since they both dry out and become waterlogged quicker than larger trees. Keep them in the shade during the hottest part of the day, and their roots need severe frost protection during winter *(see page 100)*.

HIDDEN TREASURE

One of the exciting things about this type of raw material is that you never quite know what you have got until you actually start work. In this case the initial inspection of the roots, in order to find the best viewing angle, revealed a mass of fairly thick roots growing like a spider's legs from one side of the trunk's base. The original intention was to create an informal upright or semi-cascade style, but these roots are too good to hide, so neagari it is!

1 *This healthy little spruce can be worked on at any time during spring and early summer.*

2 *Clear the debris and fine shoots from the trunk and branches.*

3 *Next, some of the low branches are pruned away to leave a clearly defined trunk. This lets light to the inner foliage and 'ages' the tree.*

4 *Potting the tree at this stage will help you to judge the proportions more easily.*

5 *Further trimming is needed, to remove more unwanted branches and to clean fine growth from the bases of the remaining branches.*

6 *The only wiring necessary is on the major branches, which need to be brought down to a horizontal plane, imparting the illusion of age.*

7 *The crown of any tree is more vigorous than the lower parts, so this needs extra thinning.*

8 *Finally, any fine, exposed hair roots should be cut away, as they are likely to wither anyway. Any shoots which grow down from the foliage pads will also need to be carefully trimmed off with the scissors.*

Below: *Only basic wiring was necessary to style this tree. In time new buds will form along the tops of all the foliage pads, giving them a domed outline. These will need to be thinned out periodically.*

ROOT OVER ROCK

One of the most dramatic of all bonsai styles echoes a tree's struggle for survival in the harsh terrain of the mountains, where the roots have had to weave their way between the rocks in search of water and nutrients.

Over the years the scarce soil becomes eroded to expose the root formation clinging tightly to the host rock. In bonsai, as in nature, this process takes many years to complete, but if done with skill and care the result is well worth waiting for.

It is essential to take your time in selecting the right materials for your creation. The rock should be stable enough not to flake away in time. It should also have lots of fissures and cracks to accommodate the roots. The texture should be fine enough to give the impression of a larger rock, in scale with the tree.

1 *This piece of water-worn limestone is ideal for root over rock style bonsai. It has plenty of fissures and generally looks very old.*

Virtually any species of tree or shrub can be used but quicker results are achieved with fast-growing species which naturally have thick, fleshy roots, such as maples, elms, larch, and so on. Pines and junipers take longer to establish on the rock although the finished product can be stunning. You should avoid plants whose roots are slow to thicken, such as cotoneaster and azalea.

Use a deep container or, better still, plant the assembly in open ground. After the first three years the plant can be lifted and the roots which grow beyond the base of the rock can be trimmed back. It should then be replanted in a deep container. Each year from now on, at repotting time, you can remove some of the surface soil, gradually exposing the roots. At the same time you should raise the rock a little in the container. Don't rush this process. Remember that roots thicken much faster below ground than when exposed to the air – the longer you wait, the better the result. During this period you can train the trunk and branches, bearing in mind that the more you restrict the top growth, the slower the roots will develop.

2 *Mix some moist clay and fine peat to the consistency of modelling clay and press it into the fissures. This will give the roots a medium to grow through.*

3 *You may need to try several plants before you find one with suitable roots.*

4 *Position the tree easily on the side of the rock. A tree perched on top of a rock looks awkward. Press the roots into the clay-filled fissures.*

5 *Use some polythene raffia or nylon ribbon to tie the roots firmly to the rock. String or wire would cut into the roots and scar them.*

6 *Wrap the rock in polythene and secure it. This forces the roots to grow downwards.*

7 *If you are using a container, fill only about a third of it with soil to start with, so that all the roots can be buried.*

Below right: *Trident maple are excellent subjects for root over rock bonsai. This four foot giant weights several hundred-weight. The shape of the tree blends perfectly with that of the rock.*

This is in fact two trees which have become fused together. Their leaves emerge in slightly different colours in spring

8 *The top few inches can be filled with gravel to stop the roots growing upwards. When watering, allow some to run down inside the polythene.*

The rock looks like a rugged mountain

Note how the roots follow the natural sweep of the rock

WRAP-AROUNDS

Here we attach living plants to driftwood, in order to create a single unit. You can produce a fair driftwood style bonsai out of otherwise useless material. However, traditionalists despise bonsai which have been created in this manner.

The Japanese call practitioners of wrap-around techniques '*Tanuki*', or cheats, after the legendary bear who could not be trusted.

The driftwood should be sound and preserved with colourless horticultural preservative several months before you attach the plant. The label on the preservative can must say: 'Harmless to plants once solvent has evaporated', or something very similar.

If the driftwood has an unstable base you can bed it in a pad of glass-fibre resin, cement or car filler paste, leaving space for the trunk and roots of the plants to fit closely to the wood. Make sure the pad will not obscure any future drainage holes.

The plants will be undergoing considerable surgery, so they need to be healthy and vigorous. Trunks must be thick enough to survive being split or shaved, half an inch at the very least, but not so thick that it cannot blend with the contours of the driftwood. Because this technique also involves root disturbance, it is best to do it in late spring.

It will take anything from four to ten years of vigorous growth for the living trunk to spread and become firmly attached to the driftwood. During this time you should replace the raffia or tape annually to avoid scarring the bark. Avoid the temptation to see how it is doing by trying to pick it away from the driftwood. If it comes away now you will have to start all over again!

N.B. Never use ferrous metal on junipers. A reaction between the metal and the sap causes decay around the wound. This reaction spreads and rapidly kills the tree.

Above: *This very old driftwood style needle juniper is the genuine article, but it gives you a good idea of the kind of image you can create given enough time.*

1 *The raw materials. The driftwood is an old, preserved Christmas tree. The plants are Blaauws junipers.*

2 *First carefully split or shave the trunk to form a flat surface which fits flush to the driftwood.*

3 *Test the progress of the work as you go, and make adjustments as necessary. It is important that the cut surface fits the driftwood closely.*

4 *Temporarily attach the plant in position with wire, and drill pilot holes through the trunk and into the driftwood, every two or three inches.*

5 *Now firmly fix the plant to the driftwood using solid brass screws,* ***never*** *steel or plated screws.*

6 *Drive the screws through the bark to hold the plant firm. The heads will heal over in a year or two. You may need to carve the driftwood to ensure a good fit.*

7 *Next, bind the plant tightly with waterproof tape. I use nylon taffeta – it is strong and does not rot. This encourages the trunk to spread sideways as it grows, so it will grip the driftwood more effectively.*

Right: *Plant the tree in a large pot to encourage rapid development. Do this work in spring, so the plants start to recover straight away, and have a full growing season ahead.*

THREAD GRAFTING

Thread grafting is a useful technique for the enthusiastic amateur bonsai grower. It is a good method for enhancing characterless trees and enables one to place new branches and foliage exactly where they are required.

1 *Test the shoots you want to use for the thread graft to make sure they are long enough and supple enough to be positioned accurately without snapping.*

This is the only type of grafting I would recommend for the amateur. For some reason it is seldom used in conventional horticulture, which is surprising because it is so easy to do and nearly always works.

Its most simple application is in creating new branches to improve a bonsai's design. If you are really ambitious you can graft an entire branch structure of a variety with, say, attractive leaves or flowers onto a more interesting trunk of a different variety which does not have these desirable characteristics. Needless to say, both branches and trunk must be of the same species.

The tree shown here has a fairly interesting trunk and root spread but has no branches at all until the very top. So we will use the thread grafting technique to create new branches exactly where we want them. The tree has been prepared by allowing a good supply of long supple shoots to grow.

2 *Very carefully drill a hole through the trunk, exactly where you want the new branch to grow. Make the hole slightly wider than the shoot.*

3 *Prepare each shoot by cutting off all the leaves at the base of the petiole. Pulling them off may damage the tender shoot at this stage. Take care not to damage the tiny buds in the axils.*

4 *Thread the shoot through the hole in the trunk until it is a tight fit, or as far as it will go without snapping. Take care not to knock off any buds.*

5 *Seal the hole either side of the trunk to prevent moisture loss, which would cause the edges of the wound to recede, taking longer to heal.*

THREAD GRAFTING ROOTS

You can use the same technique to graft on new roots. The hole is drilled at the base of the trunk and the stem of a healthy seedling or rooted cutting is passed through it. The roots of the seedling are planted in the host tree's container. Once the graft has taken, the top portion of the stem is cut away, and the lower part becomes a new surface root. The root to the right of the picture was grafted in this way.

6 *You can graft on as many branches as you like in one session.*

Below: *When you are sure the graft has been successful, you can sever each shoot where it enters the trunk and seal all the cuts. Protect the tree from strong sun and spray it daily for a few weeks.*

7 *After several months' vigorous growth the graft has taken, as shown by the thick exiting shoot.*

HELP!

SITING YOUR BONSAI

The choice of site for your bonsai display will depend largely on the layout of your garden, but it is important to consider your bonsai's requirements as well. Although different species prefer different conditions, it will help if you can keep all your collection in the same part of the garden in order to make daily watering and inspection a lot easier.

Conifers generally love to be in full sun all day and can even tolerate the heating of the pot and soil. Some tough deciduous species, such as elm, birch and hawthorn, also enjoy the sun but prefer their roots to be kept cooler, by the shade from other trees.

Species with more delicate foliage, like Japanese maples, hornbeam and beech need to be protected from strong winds as well as sun. Azaleas also suffer from over-exposure to wind and sun, but do not require full shade.

***Above:** The insulated polycarbonate wall of a greenhouse makes an ideal backdrop for bonsai, as this one at Herons Nursery. Note how the* suiseki *(viewing stones) add interest.*

***Below:** Wooden trellis is less effective as a backdrop, but does provide dappled shade. The smaller trees are protected from the strong sun by the larger ones.*

Bonsai growing in small pots will all need a certain amount of shade, regardless of the species. Small pots heat up quickly, cooking the roots and drying the soil. A permanent shadery featuring a slatted roof eliminating fifty percent of the sunlight is ideal.

Keep all bonsai on tables or custom-built benches – never on the ground. Every pest known to the gardener: slugs, ants, cats and even kids will conspire to destroy your collection in no time. Besides this, when your trees are displayed at eye-level you can appreciate them much more and will be able to spot pests and diseases a lot sooner. Benches should have slatted surfaces to allow air to circulate around the trees and the water to drain away.

Leave plenty of space between the trees so the lower branches receive light and air. Move them around occasionally so each side of the trees receive their fair share of sun. Large bonsai can be stood on 'monkey poles' – stout wooden posts with a platform fixed to the top.

Above: *This is my own back yard. The shadery filters the sun during the afternoon, while the bigger trees on benches receive full sun all day. In really wet weather I drape a plastic sheet over the shadery to prevent waterlogging of the pots. Most of the materials are second-hand, the most expensive items being the pierced bricks supporting the benches.*

Left: *Displays which are open to the public need to be protected from curious visitors by a discreet rail. Paving slabs set in coarse gravel guide the viewer along the display. Two trees are temporarily placed on the gravel, in the shade of a cedar tree, while they recover from repotting.*

FEEDING AND WATERING

The main aim of bonsai is to create a tree-like form in miniature. This can be anything from a precise replica of a classic parkland beech to the image of a gnarled and weather-beaten mountain-top juniper, which can be almost abstract in its design.

FEEDING

This can be a source of much confusion for the novice, but the principle is really quite simple. There are three ways to apply fertiliser: by placing pellets on or in the soil, by watering it onto the soil and by spraying it on the leaves (foliar feeding). Each has its own pros and cons and the choice is really based on your own preference.

Fertiliser pellets Specialist bonsai fertiliser pellets are available from all nurseries. They can be either the organic variety such as rape seed cake, or inorganic. The inorganic pellets are coated in a porous membrane which allows the nutrient to pass by the process of osmosis. Both types release nutrients slowly, which means that you don't have to worry about feeding for a while. The disadvantage is that you won't be able to adjust the feeding pattern without risking over feeding, which may 'burn' the roots.

Soil application There are a large number of soluble fertilisers available in garden centres and florists, most of which are suitable. These can be routinely applied once a week or, better still, at a quarter strength with every watering. Never use a stronger solution than the manufacturers state. It is a good idea to change brand every now and then, in order to maintain a balanced diet. The disadvantage here is that the nutrients wash out of the soil quickly, so you have to be quite strict in your feeding regime. Also, during prolonged spells of very wet weather you may not be able to feed your trees since they may not need any water.

Foliar feeding Research has shown that a plant can absorb more nutrients through its leaves than through its roots. Many standard soluble fertilisers can be applied in this way as well as via the soil, while some are specifically designed to be applied in this manner. This technique is particularly useful when your bonsai has root problems or when the soil is constantly wet through heavy rain. Foliar feeds are easy to apply provided you don't do so in strong sun, otherwise the leaves may scorch. The only disadvantage is that in warm, windy weather the solution dries on the leaves too quickly and leaves a powdery deposit

NPK

These letters appear on the packs of all good fertilisers and are followed by a sequence of numbers, for example NPK 7 : 11 : 9.5. The letters are the chemical symbols for the three major nutrients and the numbers denote their ratio. The higher the numbers, the stronger the fertiliser. For bonsai it is wisest to stick with brands with weaker mixes.

So our example has seven parts of nitrogen (N), eleven parts of phosphorus (P) and nine-and-a-half parts of potassium (K). It is a fairly well-balanced feed for sustaining growth.

Any of these methods of feeding are suitable for keeping an established tree in good health and vigour, but occasionally you may need to use a specialist feed in order to encourage the tree to perform in a specific way. Before you attempt this you will need to understand a little more about how each of the major nutrients affects the tree.

This unusual and desirable clump style bonsai is Japanese holly, or Ilex serrata. *(The Japanese call it English holly!). It is encouraged to flower and fruit prolifically by a high potassium diet.*

Nitrogen This is responsible for leaf and stem growth and can enrich the colour of the foliage. Without any nitrogen a plant would only produce a few stunted leaves and growth would be poor. The plant's health would quickly deteriorate because it would not be able to carry out the process of photosynthesis efficiently.

Phosphorus This nutrient is primarily responsible for root growth. It also encourages thick, sturdy trunks, helps to strengthen the plant against disease and frosts, and promotes back-budding.

Potassium Potassium, or potash, is responsible for encouraging flowers and fruit as well as hardening off late growth before the winter. If left out of its diet, a plant will fail to flower, or if it does then the blooms will be of poor quality and the fruit will not set. Potassium also helps to build up the plant's resistance to disease.

Special feeding programmes From what we have learned above it is easy to deduce how we can use each element to produce specific results by increasing its proportion in the fertiliser. Here are some points as to why and when this should be done.

Nitrogen (N) should be increased when you want a plant to put on a spurt of rapid growth. This applies to young, developing plants which you want to grow larger before starting to train. If the foliage is dull a little extra nitrogen may improve the colour.

If you use a soluble fertiliser to enrich your plant's soil, never use a stronger solution than the manufacturers state.

A high nitrogen feed should be applied as the tree needs it, not before. So in spring, after growth has started, or once new leaves have emerged following leaf pruning, an application of a high nitrogen feed will replenish the tree's resources.

Phosphorus (P) is especially useful after repotting or when a tree is recovering from a root problem, so a little extra can be given at such times. In fact, a high phosphorus and potassium feed will aid recovery from many ailments.

Increasing the phosphorus content in the diet in late summer and autumn toughens up the tree in readiness for autumn. A pinch of powdered superphosphate on the surface of the soil is an easy method of application.

Potassium (K) should be increased for all flowering and fruiting bonsai. A diluted rose or tomato feed is ideal, as these are specifically formulated to increase the flowering and fruiting potential. Potash can also be increased to help weak plants regain strength. Extra potassium given during late summer and autumn will help the tree combat the perils of winter. A little sulphate of potash sprinkled on the soil once a week will do the trick.

Some nurseries sell a specialist soluble fertiliser called '0-10-10' which, as the name implies, is nitrogen free and is ideal for late season feeding. When buying fertilisers make sure that they include trace elements. These are only required in minute quantities but without them your bonsai will surely suffer. If you decide to use products which do not contain trace elements, you should add them separately twice a year.

Korean hornbeams naturally develop this attractive streaky bark, even in young trees

This wavy trunk line results from hard pruning the stem of a plant with alternate leaves

A spacing bar is used to hold two trunks apart until they are set in the desired position

The trunk lines of Korean hornbeams (Carpinus turczaninowii) *make them ideal for group plantings. Foliar feeding is necessary to ensure that the smaller trees receive their fair share of nourishment.*

WATERING

In theory, provided your bonsai is growing in a free-draining soil *(see page 42)* it should not be possible to over water. But many beginners, in their enthusiasm, manage to do just that. Over watering eliminates the air contained in the spaces between the soil particles and 'drowns' the roots. It also creates the conditions favoured by various root-rotting fungi. The symptoms of decaying roots (yellowing foliage and lack of new growth) are not usually apparent until the damage has already been done. However, the odd drenching now and then won't hurt. On the other hand, it is essential to prevent the soil drying out completely.

Generally the best method is to water the surface of the soil evenly, using a fine rose or spray, until the water drains out of the drainage holes. Wait a few minutes and repeat. This ensures a thorough wetting of the soil and should be sufficient for one day during the height of summer. Try to avoid watering a tree that doesn't really need it. Wind can dry the soil's surface to a crisp, while deeper in the pot it may still be quite wet. If in doubt, check by scraping away the surface in a couple of places and adjust the amount of water accordingly.

The best time to water is in early evening. This gives the tree plenty of time to have a good drink before morning. If you water in the morning, the tree doesn't have much of a chance to refresh itself before the heat of the day. If you can't avoid watering in the morning, do it as early as possible. Another advantage with evening is that you can douse the foliage at the same time without the risk of leaf scorch caused by the water droplets acting as miniature magnifying glasses in the sun. All bonsai appreciate a daily shower.

A word of warning Don't assume that the rain will do the watering for you. A bonsai acts like an umbrella, and it shelters the pot from all but the heaviest downpour. Therefore, it is well worth continuing to check the need to water even in wet weather.

Organic fertiliser pellets can be either evenly distributed on the surface, or lightly pressed into the soil. They break down with watering and release the nutrients gradually over a three month period.

Foliar feed can be applied either with a hand spray or a watering can. A spray allows localised feeding of weaker branches, in order to build up their strength.

DEALING WITH PESTS AND DISEASES

Bonsai are prone to the same diseases and pests that attack full-size trees, but because they are small and compact, it doesn't take long at all for a localised problem to spread over the entire tree, with disastrous results. And because it grows slowly, a bonsai is less able to outgrow an infection, or a plague of aphids, in the same way a full-size tree can.

Aphids, surely the most common of all pests, here shown on pine. There are many species, but all succumb readily to conventional pesticides.

Adelgids form a waxy residue on pine shoots, and can kill them. Detergent in the solution helps penetrate the waxy protection.

A twice-yearly precautionary treatment with a systemic insecticide and fungicide will help, but it will not be one hundred percent successful. (Systemic chemicals are designed to be absorbed by the plant and fight the problem from the inside). Deciduous trees will benefit from a normal garden 'winter wash'.

Constant vigilance is necessary all through the year. Once a problem has been spotted and diagnosed remedial action should be taken immediately, using an appropriate commercial treatment.

Always read the pack to make sure the treatment is effective for your particular problem, and follow the manufacturer's instructions to the letter. If one brand doesn't appear to work try another – some insects seem to be able to build up a tolerance if the same brand is used all the time.

Trees may take weeks to recover from fungal infections, so don't lose heart. If the symptoms stop getting worse, the treatment has more than likely worked.

Never use systemics on Chinese elms. They will not kill the tree but the foliage will yellow and fall and fine twigs may die back.

Scale insects come in many different sizes. These, on a Chinese juniper, are tiny and very difficult to spot.

These scale insects are easier to spot once mature. The big ones can be easily picked off.

The notorious vine weevil can devour a pot full of roots in no time. Treat soil with Gamma HCH and check soil when repotting.

***Below:** The vine weevil lays rapidly hatching, eggs. Squash on sight!*

***Left:** These streaks are caused by the leaf miner grub. It is unsightly but harmless. Remove affected foliage.*

Brown patches are caused by too-strong insecticide or the sun shining through magnifying water droplets.

Many trees are attacked by tiny mites which stimulate galls to form on the leaves, like these on elm. Removing all infected leaves in June is the only known cure.

Red spider mites are microscopic sap-sucking creatures which infest plants in vast numbers, even in mid-winter. The leaves or needles turn brown in patches, and sometimes a minute web can be detected. Cold water spray helps with control; most insecticides are effective.

***Below:** 'Pine needle cast' starts as yellowing blotches on the needles, which soon fall. This seriously damages full-size trees and can kill bonsai. Once diagnosed, treat monthly with Bordeaux mixtures or 'Zineb'.*

SPRING BONSAI MAINTENANCE

As spring gets underway, excitement mounts as your trees begin to stir. This is the beginning of the busiest season of the year, when you can do a certain amount of creative work as well as more down-to-earth tasks.

EARLY SPRING

Repotting Any healthy deciduous trees you have not been able to repot yet should be attended to in the first part of this month. If there is no sign of root or bud movement, wait a little longer. Continue to keep newly repotted trees away from hard frosts and drying winds. You can keep deciduous trees in an outhouse if necessary at this time. Until the buds open they have no need of light. However, as soon as they begin to burst you must place the tree outside. Don't wire newly repotted trees for three or four weeks, thus avoiding strain on the emerging new roots. Towards the end of the month you can begin to repot junipers and spruces.

Pruning Deciduous trees can be pruned once the buds begin to show signs of activity. Seal all wounds. Thin out the fine twigs on deciduous trees so the coming season's growth won't outgrow the design. Remember to prune to a side shoot or to a bud which is pointing in the direction you want new growth.

Wiring Start wiring most deciduous trees – fine twigs as well as thick branches – before the buds swell if possible. If the buds have

Because this book will be read in both the north and south hemispheres, we refer to the months in this section as parts of a season, rather than by name. The table below gives the equivalent month in both hemispheres.

Northern Hemisphere	Month	Southern Hemisphere
Early spring	March	Early autumn
Mid-spring	April	Mid-autumn
Late spring	May	Late autumn
Early summer	June	Early winter
Mid-summer	July	Mid-winter
Late summer	August	Late winter
Early autumn	September	Early spring
Mid-autumn	October	Mid-spring
Late autumn	November	Late spring
Early winter	December	Early summer
Mid-winter	January	Mid-summer
Late winter	February	Late summer

already started to move take extra care as they are easily dislodged at this crucial stage in their development. Leave three weeks between wiring and repotting.

Watering Keep soil just moist. Be especially careful not to allow newly-repotted trees to become too wet. Place them under shelter during rainy spells if necessary.

Feeding Do not feed newly repotted trees until the buds are open. Trees in training which are not being repotted may benefit from a little bonemeal or fish emulsion.

MID-SPRING

Repotting If you haven't finished repotting deciduous trees, it is best to leave them for next year unless they are really rootbound.

Pruning Now you can prune with a little more confidence, since the buds will be opening and you can spot any dead branches or twigs. Seal all wounds.

Wiring Wire spruce, juniper and pine but not deciduous trees. Don't wire too tightly because the branches will thicken rapidly for the next month or so.

Watering During rainy spells shelter newly repotted trees, but you may need to water daily in dry weather.

Feeding Don't fertilise newly repotted trees. Those repotted last month can be given their first spring feed if growth has properly started.

LATE SPRING

Repotting All repotting should be finished by the first week. Only repot in emergencies, such as newly-detected root rot.

Pruning Trees in training can be pruned now but you should already have finished all your deciduous display trees.

Wiring Conifers can now be wired, but take care not to damage the new growth. On deciduous trees, new shoots may also be teased into position by delicate wiring.

Trimming Pinch out expanding pine candles as they grow. Start with the small ones and finish with the larger ones a week or so later. Spruce and juniper may also be ready for their first bout of pinching. New growth on early deciduous trees will need to be trimmed back to two or three buds. Also rub off any unwanted adventitious buds so no energy is wasted.

Watering Now the trees are in full swing they will need watering at least once a day, but not in full sun if you can help it. Spray the foliage as you go.

Feeding Late developers can be given a little extra nitrogen, others should now be receiving a balanced diet on a regular basis. Don't feed any trees which have not yet

As the weather warms, the tiny bright red leaves of this Acer palmatum 'deshojo' *emerge.*

SUMMER BONSAI MAINTENANCE

As summer begins, new foliage is hardening off and flowering is now over. You and your trees settle into a routine which will last for the next three months.

EARLY SUMMER

Repotting Only Chinese junipers can be repotted with confidence now provided they are kept sheltered from drying winds and full sun for a while. Trees which appear too large for their current containers now that they have grown a little can be planted in larger pots provided the roots are not damaged.

Pruning Start to prune pines and spruce now. Deciduous trees can also be pruned now, but they are likely to throw out vigorous shoots from around the wound.

Trimming Keep at it. Some trees will have a pause in growth towards the end of the month and a second surge later. This later growth will appear at the tips of the earlier shoots unless they are trimmed back.

Wiring Wire anything that takes your fancy. Check wire applied earlier in the year.

Watering At least once a day. Spray the foliage as you water, but not in strong sun as this will scorch the leaves.

Feeding Give regular balanced feeds.

MID-SUMMER

Pruning Wounds will heal quickly at this time of year. A good time to prune pines, but beware of over-pruning deciduous trees; it is difficult to see the structure through the leaves and you may be making a mistake. This is a good time to create sharis.

Trimming Carry on as last month where necessary. Junipers will be racing away now and will need a lot of attention. Leaf prune up to the middle of the month.

Wiring Wire away, especially conifers.

Watering Carry on as last month, only more so. It is by now especially important to water in the early evening if possible.

__Below:__ This dramatic little literati style hawthorn was created almost entirely by pruning, from a much larger bush which I rescued from a condemned hedgerow.

HOLIDAY CARE

There are any number of contrivances intended to water your trees for you for two weeks. They include felt wicks trailing from the pot into a bucket, enclosing pot and tree in a polythene bag, and more sophisticated apparatus like automatically-timed sprinklers. None of them are foolproof and there are nearly always some fatalities. If you try any of these the worry will only spoil your holiday.

The best thing to do is give a friendly neighbour (or, better still, a bonsai colleague) the undoubted privilege of caring for your trees while you are away. Ask them to come round a couple of times before your go away, to have a practice run. Many nurseries offer a holiday-care service which is usually quite inexpensive, and is often free.

If neither of these options are possible, remove the trees from their pots and plant them in a shady corner, burying the root mass a few inches deep and taking care not to damage the roots. Water the area well before and after planting. The only other alternative is to do what I do: stay home and take your holiday in winter, like your trees.

Feeding As last month. Give high potash feeds to flowering bonsai.

LATE SUMMER

Pruning Wounds heal quickly if pruning is carried out by the middle of the month. Heavy pruning may result in new growth which will not harden off before winter.

Trimming This is becoming progressively less necessary now, with the exception of junipers, which will be steaming away for a while yet, on into the next couple of months. Don't leaf prune this month.

Wiring Wire applied now to deciduous species is unlikely to have much effect until growth starts next year. However, it is certainly still a good time to wire conifers, especially junipers.

Watering This is just as hectic as last month. Make sure that pots which become very dry are thoroughly soaked. When the soil has become a little compacted, water will often wet the surface and run down the inside of the pot without passing through it. If you suspect this might be happening, dunk the pot in the bath for half an hour to give it a thorough drenching.

Feeding Reduce the amount of nitrogen that you give this month, eliminating it completely during the last week.

In the full flush of summer, this clump-style Japanese maple needs constant attention. Shoots must be pinched almost daily to keep it in trim.

AUTUMN BONSAI MAINTENANCE

Growth slows to a standstill this month. Roots and buds harden, seeds are dispersed, and inner leaves begin to fall. Sunny days and colder nights induce the first hints of autumn colour. You can begin to relax a little.

EARLY AUTUMN

Pruning Only pines, if you must. Deciduous trees may still be boosted into growth, which will not harden in time for winter and will be nipped off by the first frost.

Trimming Not necessary now – except for those persistent junipers, which will carry on growing for another month or so. Frost will make the newly-pinched shoots turn brown, so be aware.

Wiring Not advisable. Without new growth the branches are unlikely to set and any fractures in the bark may allow frost to enter over winter, risking damage.

Watering As your trees begin to slow down, so can you. Be vigilant, though – changeable weather can deceive you, and pots can still dry out surprisingly quickly.

Feeding Be sure to give plenty of nitrogen-free fertiliser all month. Additional bonemeal can be applied to pines, whose roots remain slightly active all winter, and will be appreciated by them early next year.

General This is the last chance to do any jins or sharis while the sap is still on the move. Next month the bark will be more stubborn to remove, and the wounds will not begin to heal until spring. Pests are less of a problem now than they are in spring and summer, but some are still active on conifers. Sow collected seeds in trays outdoors. Remove debris from both the tree and the surface of the soil to prevent disease.

This is a good time to plant new moss. It will continue to grow during mild spells all winter and will have taken hold by next spring. Limit the moss to the area around the roots. A total covering will harbour pests and will also prevent inspection of the soil.

This Japanese hornbeam, in common with its European cousin and most beeches, naturally retains its dead leaves all winter to protect the buds from frost.

MID-AUTUMN

'Season of mists and mellow fruitfulness'. Red and gold leaves speckled with dew. Put your feet up and enjoy it.

Wiring Remove all tight wire by carefully cutting it away from the branches. Don't attempt to re-apply if it involves additional bending of the branch until next spring.

Watering Only when necessary. For the next two months pots can still dry out but mists and dew may make the surface appear wet, while the soil below may be quite dry. By now you should be able to judge how dry the pot is by the weight.

General Good hygiene is essential – clean debris from trees and pots. Keep an eye open for plants to dig up for future training. Take hardwood cuttings and sow hard-shelled collected seed outdoors. Start planning your winter protection.

LATE AUTUMN

The last leaves of autumn fall, to reveal the fine tracery twigs your summer-long trimming has produced. Rich, green conifers sparkle with frost. A time to contemplate your bonsai with satisfaction, and appreciate the fruits of your labour.

Repotting Raw material can be dug up and potted into large containers or growing beds, if the species is fully hardy. Large, fully hardy deciduous bonsai can be repotted now, but only if the roots can be protected from hard frost all winter.

Pruning Only rough pruning of raw material is necessary. Even well-sealed wounds may die back around the edges over winter if the weather is severe enough. It is advisable to leave short stubs as a precautionary measure. These can be trimmed off next spring.

Wiring It is tempting to work on your trees when the branches are clear and the structure can be seen. But wiring now will encourage die-back, and may well lead to disappointment.

Watering Do this only when necessary, but check every couple of days. Wind can dry pots almost as quickly as the sun. The greatest danger, though, is over watering, especially in periods of rainy weather.

General Continue clearing general debris, especially dead annual mosses, and any leaves which are caught up in the twigs (leave the dead leaves on beech and hornbeams). These may harbour pests and fungal spores. Prepare your tree's winter quarters by cleaning thoroughly and spraying with insecticide and fungicide. Check every tree for persistent pests such as scale insect, galls, etc., and inspect conifers for signs of spider mite. Treat trees with a non-systemic fungicide as a precaution. Take hardwood cuttings, and sow hard-shelled seeds.

Once this ten-inch tall, formal upright English elm has shed its leaves, the beauty of its fine twigs can be fully appreciated.

WINTER BONSAI MAINTENANCE

In winter, nature shuts up shop and takes a well-earned rest – but when it comes to your bonsai, you still have work to do.

EARLY WINTER

Repotting Finish potting up all newly-collected raw material by the middle of the month, and protect the roots from the worst of the weather.

Pruning Only rough pruning of any raw material is safe now. Leave short stubs which can be trimmed off in spring.

Wiring Tempting, but resist.

Watering Keep soil moist if the weather doesn't do it for you. Waterlogging can be a problem with trees exposed all winter. Use your discretion, and shelter trees if necessary during prolonged spells of heavy rain.

General All trees which require winter protection should be fully accommodated by the middle of the month. Thoroughly clean the trees first and spray them with non-systemic fungicide, if you forgot to do it last month. Photograph your trees for a record as you put them away, as a matter of routine. Hardwood cuttings may still be successful if taken this month.

MID-WINTER

Watering Trees kept in the open will not need watering – in fact they may even need to be protected from excessive rain. A thick blanket of snow does no harm to large, hardy trees in the open. But if the thaw is rapid, the trees are likely to receive the equivalent of a week's rain in just one day, so it is wise to clear the snow before this happens. Trees under cover should be inspected weekly and kept just moist.

General Inspect trees for pests during your weekly water check. Conifers under cover can be devastated by aphids or spider mites at any time during the winter, in a matter of a couple of weeks. Also check the peat boxes you plunged your smaller trees in and clean off any moss.

LATE WINTER

Repotting Truly hardy deciduous trees can be repotted towards the end of the month if the roots are white at the tips. Protect them from hard frost and heavy rain until the buds start to open. Don't feed until spring. Raw

Large, hardy conifer plantings, like this Edo spruce group, actually prefer to be exposed to the rigours of winter.

material can be dug from the ground and potted into temporary growing containers.

Pruning You can begin to prune hardy deciduous trees if you are sure the remaining shoots and branches are in good health. Seal wounds and protect from frost until growth has started. Towards the end of the month, last year's shoots and old spurs can be trimmed back to live buds *(see page 56)*.

Wiring Wire deciduous trees while the buds are still tight against the shoots. As the buds swell they become more fragile and are easily damaged and even more easily dislodged. Don't wait too long or you will get caught out.

Watering Keep repotted trees moist but not wet. Shelter them from constant rain. Other trees will begin to demand water as they come out of dormancy

Feeding Feeding now might damage delicate young roots. Trees which have already started to move, and conifers which did not receive their bonemeal last autumn, can be helped along with a dose of fish emulsion, which is very gentle on the roots.

General Sudden attacks of aphids or spider mites can defoliate conifers within a week or two, so keep a careful watch. Clean algae from trunks, and remove all scale insects you may find. Take small trees from their peat boxes and return them to their pots. Don't root prune them just yet. Preserve timber benches if you haven't already done so. Plan your workload for the next two, busy months.

Hardy bonsai, like hardy trees in the wild, may spend weeks under a blanket of snow, and come to no harm. The snow maintains an even temperature in the pot and prevents transpiration.

WINTER PROTECTION

Most fully hardy species tolerate having their pots frozen solid for short periods at a time. Pines and spruces even seem to thrive on this treatment, preferring it to just about any form of protection at all. But the ravages of winter can take their toll on most other species in a number of ways.

All the effects discussed below can damage a large bonsai but it should survive. Medium-size bonsai – say between ten and eighteen inches tall – can be severely damaged, possibly fatally, while small bonsai are very vulnerable indeed.

Constant freezing and thawing of the pot every day can devastate a root system, especially if the pot never entirely thaws before re-freezing. The root tips absorb moisture but cannot pass it through the frozen roots in the centre of the pot. On re-freezing they expand and burst, just like a water pipe. They can also be crushed by the pressure caused by the expansion of rapidly freezing soil in a container. Remember a waterlogged soil expands more on freezing than a comfortably moist one.

Good hygiene is essential. Pick off dead leaves, which harbour pests and diseases over winter. At the same time, pick off any scale insects that you find on the tree.

Although roots are inactive most of the time during winter, moisture is still lost through the bark of the tree. Under normal circumstances the tree would contain enough reserves and the roots could replenish the supply during mild weather.

Cold, drying winds can desiccate fine twigs. Frozen roots cannot replenish the moisture so the twigs die back.

Wind and sun can cause pots to dry out, even in winter.

Saturated soil not only increases the risk of frost damage – it also creates the ideal environment for root rot.

Protective measures Despite all the dangers your bonsai have to face, let me assure you that by taking a few simple precautions you can guarantee them a long

It is a good idea to peel away surface moss, which can harbour insect pests and fungal spores. This is essential on small bonsai which are going to be buried in peat.

and happy life. There are five basic ways to site your bonsai over winter, each offering them a different degree of protection: (1) *Open:* Trees are left on benches which are protected from severe wind by a nearby fence or outhouse. (2) *Wind protection:* Pots are stood on bricks or boxes between the benches. If the benches run east/west, place a board at the eastern end to prevent a wind-tunnel effect. (3) *Shelter:* A covered area, closed on three sides and open on the fourth, preferably western side. The easiest solution is to place the trees on bricks under the benches. Cover the benches with clear polythene and weight it down securely on three sides. In really severe weather the fourth side can be closed off temporarily. Pots should be inspected regularly for dryness. If well constructed, this type of shelter can also double as winter confinement. (4) *Winter confinement:* This involves protecting the tree against wind, sun, rain and rapid temperature change. It doesn't offer a totally frost-free environment as this would disturb dormancy in hardy trees. Deciduous trees can be kept in a shed or garage – they need no light until spring. The ideal environment for all trees is a polythene greenhouse, or polytunnel, which can be opened at both ends to allow an air change. To prevent rapid changes in temperature, the polytunnel should be shaded from strong sun. Inspect trees regularly for dryness and insect attack. (5) *Frost-free:* If you are not sure about the hardiness of an unusual species then it is as well to keep it in a cool conservatory or unheated room through the winter.

Guide to Winter Protection

Large Bonsai

- Pines and spruces – open
- Juniper – open, give blue-leaved varieties wind protection
- Very hardy species (English elm, field maple, larch, etc.) – wind protection. Shelter from prolonged rain
- Hardy species (Japanese maples, ornamentals) – shelter
- Temperamental plants (red maples, spring flowering varieties) – shelter
- Trident maples and Chinese elm – winter confinement

Medium size bonsai

- Pines and spruces – open, wind protection in very severe weather
- Junipers, very hardy species – wind protection, shelter in harsh weather
- Hardy species – shelter from rain
- Temperamental plants, tridents and Chinese elms – winter confinement

Small bonsai

- Pines and spruces – wind protection
- Junipers, very hardy and hardy species – winter confinement. Remove smaller trees from their pots and bury them in boxes of damp peat
- Temperamental plants, tridents and Chinese elms – winter confinement, small trees packed in peat boxes. Keep trees just above freezing.

Small bonsai should be gently teased from their pots and plunged into a box of loose peat. Cover the moss with a one-inch layer of loose peat to insulate it.

An ideal impromptu bonsai shelter. A considerable number of trees can be packed in the spaces below the benches and the whole thing covered in heavy-duty polythene. During spells of really severe weather, the front of this shelter is rolled down for extra protection, and the trident maple and Chinese elm are brought into a cold, but frost-free, outhouse.

Classic Bonsai Styles & Plants

CLASSIC BONSAI STYLES

There is an infinite variety of tree shapes in nature which are imitated in bonsai. It would be impractical, even impossible, to name all of the many styles individually, so over the centuries the Japanese devised a number of general classifications.

Over a period of time, the Japanese formalised their general classifications and defined a number of classic styles for bonsai, each having its own aesthetic rules. These many and various rules govern the shape, angle and proportion of the trunk, number of trunks and location of branches, and so on, for all types of tree.

Although it is only very rarely possible to follow these rules to the letter, tradition states that they should be aspired to at all times. Having said this, it is also true that many of the most admired bonsai in the world break the rules in some way.

I personally prefer a more relaxed and inspirational approach to bonsai, reflecting the more liberal western approach to life in general. However, the rules governing the classic styles are extremely useful to know, since they enable bonsai enthusiasts to describe their trees to one another, and they help the beginner to create an aesthetically pleasing design without unnecessary frustration.

Once you have gained a little experience you can break the rules at will and let your own creativity run free.

***Below:** This stunning informal upright Black pine* (Pinus thunbergii)*, owned by Peter Chan, is a classic example of the style. Note the off-centre placement in the pot.*

One of the outstanding features of this tree is the strong surface root formation

FORMAL UPRIGHT

直幹

CHOKKAN

As the name implies, this is the most formalised of all styles. The trunk must be ramrod straight and bolt upright, tapering uniformly from base to tip. The branches should be arranged alternately either side of the trunk with every third branch to the rear. The branches should diminish in thickness and in length from the lowest one upwards, and should be either horizontal or sloping downwards. Ideally, the spaces between the branches should also diminish toward the top of the tree, in proportion to their thickness and length.

INFORMAL UPRIGHT

模様木

MOYOGI

This is a variation on the formal upright style but is much easier to create. The rules for the branch structure are the same but the trunk may have any number of curves, both from left to right and from front to back. The branches should ideally grow from the outside of the curves and never on the inside as this creates a shock to the eye. The apex should lean towards the front. The tree illustrated is just one of the many variations on the informal upright style. Unlike the Formal Upright, Moyogi works equally as well with deciduous and coniferous species.

SLANTING

斜幹

SHAKAN

Another variation on the formal upright style, except that it is not upright. The trunk is usually straight-ish, although it may have a gentle curve or two. The placement of the branches needs to be carefully thought out in order to stabilise the design and to prevent the tree looking as if it is about to fall over. Unlike the previous two styles, the number and placement of the branches is less crucial, providing the opportunity for creativity. For instance, using only the top branches and training them down steeply can result in a dramatic image.

WINDSWEPT

吹流

FUKINAGASHI

Although this is one of the more naturalistic styles, it is also one of the most dramatic. The aim is to capture the dynamic shape and movement of a tree living high in the mountains or on a clifftop, where it is constantly exposed to high prevailing winds. There are no rules governing the trunk shape or location of branches, but in spite of this freedom this is one of the most difficult styles to create successfully. The difficulty lies in making the image appear authentic, rather than merely looking like a tree with branches on one side. The trick is to ensure that the windswept effect begins at the base of the trunk and is reflected in every aspect of the tree.

SEMI-CASCADE

半懸崖

HAN-KENGAI

Both this style and the cascade style depict trees clinging to a cliff face, where they are beaten by snow, wind and rockfalls. The trunk should have dramatic curves and taper, and the branches should ideally also cascade from the trunk. Tradition states that the inverted 'apex' should be positioned directly below the base of the trunk when the tree is viewed from the 'front', but this can inhibit the design somewhat. These days it's perfectly acceptable to allow the lowest point of the tree to be placed to one side of the pot, as if it was reaching out from a cliff face to find light. The one unbreakable rule is that the lowest point must be below the rim of the pot, but not its base.

CASCADE

懸崖

KENGAI

The difference between this style and the semi-cascade is that here the trunk must fall below the base of the pot. All other criteria are the same. Good cascades are rare because of the difficulty in maintaining vigour in the lower parts of the tree, opposing its natural urge to grow upwards. This is probably the most difficult of all styles to design convincingly, partly because of the horticultural problem, but mainly because we have few natural examples to recall as inspiration. It is important to include dramatic features and sharp angles to evoke the feeling of a tree clinging to life in the harsh mountain conditions.

DRIFTWOOD

娑婆幹

SHARIMIKI

Echoing the natural appearance of mountain junipers, which produce areas of bare, sun-bleached wood as they age, this style is seldom successfully created from other species. The focal point is the beautiful and dramatic shapes of the grain in the exposed wood. These shapes may be natural but are more often elaborately carved and then bleached and preserved with lime-sulphur. The foliage masses, although acknowledging some of the rules of other styles, serve more as a foil or frame to the driftwood. This style is suitable for conifers and rarely, if ever, applied to deciduous species of bonsai tree.

A high potash fertiliser encourages flowers and fruit

Roots need to be buried for many years to become as thick as these

***Left:** Pyracantha make very attractive bonsai, especially when the rather feminine beauty of the flowers and fruit are contrasted with the more masculine styles like cascade or this root-over-rock.*

BROOM

姿婆幹

HÔKIDACHI

This style was modelled on the natural habit of the zelkova and is seldom successfully used for other than related species, since it works best with trees bearing alternate foliage. All branches should emerge from the top of a straight trunk and fork at regularly diminishing internals until a network of fine shoots at the tips forms an even-domed crown. For broom styles to work well, they must be perfectly symmetrical and meticulously trained and pruned to ensure an even and gradual transition from trunk, through heavy branches, to the finest terminal shoots. Trying to rush the development will always end in disappointment.

LITERATI

文 人 木

BUNJINGI

This style is reminiscent of ancient pines, which tend to shed their lower branches as they get old. It gets its name from the calligraphic style of ancient Chinese artists. The focal point of the design is the trunk, so it should be full of character. The branches are limited to the uppermost part of the trunk and should bear just enough foliage to keep the tree healthy and vigorous. The foliage should, however, be immaculately positioned. The pots used for literati styles are generally round and comparatively small to balance the sparse foliage. They are also frequently 'rustic' in appearance, to reflect the tree's rocky habitat.

ROOT-OVER-ROCK

石上樹

SEKIJÔJU

In rocky terrain the scarce soil is constantly being eroded, exposing the rocks and the roots of the trees growing amongst them. This style depicts such a tree whose roots, as they thicken, cling to any rocks beneath them. The tree itself can be of any style, although broom and formal upright styles look out of place. The most important factor is that the roots should cling tightly to the rock and should have a mature texture. This can take many years to accomplish. First, the root-covered rock must first be planted in the ground for several seasons to consolidate, and then exposed to the air and sun for the bark to develop mature characteristics.

ROOT-ON-ROCK

石付

ISHITSUKI

The tree itself may follow any style, the significance is that a rock is used instead of a pot, with the roots growing in a crevice or hollow. The rock may stand in a shallow dish of soil or, better still, in a water tray. Mixed plantings of pines with red maples or dwarf quince and azalea are particularly successful The essence of the root on rock style is the natural landscape that the composition evokes. The choice of rocks, tree species and various accompanying plants must be carefully made, ensuring that they all harmonise visually and horticulturally, since repotting can be a difficult operation.

SINUOUS RAFT

根連

NETSUNANARI

As the name suggests, this is a raft planting where the original horizontal trunk has attractive snake-like curves and is exposed in such a way as to show this feature to its best advantage. With a style like this it is even acceptable for the old trunk to be above the ground in places. The natural inspiration for the sinuous raft style is a fallen tree that has sprouted vertical branches and then taken root in places where it has come into contact with the earth. Although trees of this kind themselves may conform to any style, they should harmonise and all be similar in trunk movement.

STRAIGHT RAFT

筏吹

IKADABUKI

Another obvious one: a raft planting where the original trunk lies in a straight line. Most rafts created from nursery stock follow this style because of the difficulty of bending a fairly thick trunk into sinuous curves. In such cases the trunk is usually buried in the soil or covered with moss to disguise its unnatural appearance. The main problem to solve when making a straight raft is how to avoid a straight row of trunks. This can be achieved by training some branches horizontally forward or backward before bending them up to form trunks. It is even possible to create a fairly dense forest in this way.

EXPOSED ROOT

根上

NEAGARI

Most of us have driven down lanes where the steep banks have been washed away to expose the roots of an ancient beech or pine, and this style is based on such cases. The roots, which must have mature bark and interesting shapes, add a dramatic, rugged appearance, so the design of the tree itself should echo this. The foliage mass should be kept fairly small so that its weight or wind resistance doesn't cause the exposed roots to bend over. You might find wild specimens that lend themselves to training in this style, but more often than not, growing from scratch is the easiest method.

TWIN TRUNK

雙樹

SÔJU

Two trunks, one smaller than the other, joined together at the base. Trunks which divide significantly above the base are unacceptable. The smaller or secondary trunk should be slightly to the rear of the dominant one to enhance the perspective. The trees themselves may follow any appropriate style. These bonsai can sometimes be difficult to maintain in the long term, because as the trunks thicken with age, the fork between them inevitably begins to fill. This has the effect of raising the junction until eventually it is too high. When starting a *sôju*, make the angle between the trunks as wide as possible.

TWISTED TRUNK

蟠幹

BANKAN

This most unnatural of all bonsai styles has heavy Chinese influence. It became popular for a time last century and was grown in large numbers. Although still popular among some hobbyists, it is seldom accepted in classic circles. The trunk spirals from base to apex while the branch structure follows that of the informal upright. Unfortunately, the majority of commercial, mass-produced small bonsai – intended for the gift market – are bad examples of this style. Far Eastern growers seem to think that this is what Westerners believe a tree looks like!

CLUMP

株立

KABUDACHI

Any (odd) number of trunks, which must be in a variety of sizes, all growing on the same roots. This may either be created from suckers (shoots arising naturally from the roots) or by cutting off a thick trunk at the base and using the new shoots which spring up from the stump. The trees can be any style. The horticultural advantage of using a clump rather than separate plants is that the 'trees' do not compete for water and nutrients. As with the raft and group styles, the trunks should have similar movement and characteristics but must also vary in thickness.

GROUP

寄植

YOSE-UE

This style may incorporate any number of trunks from seven up to as many as you like. The main interest is in the interplay between the trunks, which should be of different sizes and should be arranged to give the impression of depth and perspective. No three trunks should form a straight line and no trunk should be obscured by another when viewed from the front. The trees in the centre of the group or forest should be the tallest, with the thickest trunks bearing the most foliage. The trunks on the perimeter should lean outward, reaching for the light.

BREAK THE RULES

This clump-style Japanese red maple breaks one rule by having an even number of trunks. Nevertheless, it is a fine example.

GARDEN CENTRE PLANTS: COTONEASTER

One of my favourite species for bonsai is Cotoneaster. The tiny leaves are dark, glossy green, they bear minute pink-white flowers in spring and the bright red berries stay on the plant from late summer right through the winter.

Some varieties of cotoneaster, like *horizontalis*, which we have chosen here, are deciduous, giving the added bonus of autumn golds and reds. The growth is symmetrical and entirely predictable, producing a herring-bone pattern of branches and twigs – ideal for bonsai training into almost any style.

Garden centre plants tend to be well fed and watered but they live

1 *This cotoneaster is typical of garden centre stock, with its strong branches.*

2 *The essence of a good cascade style is to make the trunk begin its cascade as close to the base as possible, so it is cut right back to the lowest pair of heavy branches.*

fairly close together. This tends to encourage long, vigorous shoots which we are going to use to our advantage in this exercise by creating a cascade style.

Because it is against the tree's nature to grow downwards, it will channel more energy to the crown at the expense of the tip of the cascade. To compensate for this you should select a vigorous branch for the

3 *One remaining branch becomes the new leader and the other is shortened to form a low, stunted crown.*

4 *Rub off cluttered shoots and wire the new trunk from base to tip.*

5 *Make the bends in the trunk sharp, reflecting the tortuous conditions suffered in nature.*

6 *Leave a few short stubs to serve as anchorage points for the wire when you prune.*

7 *Once the tree is planted in a proper cascade pot the final adjustments can be made to the branches. It will now grow away vigorously, especially at the extreme top and bottom, so regular pruning will be needed to keep the foliage pads neat. In time more branches may be pruned.*

The deep pot creates a visual and horticultural balance

Cascade style bonsai need to be displayed on tall stands, such as this rosewood one from China

Garden Centre Plants: Cedar

The Literati style, although found frequently in nature, gets its name from the fact that the trunk shapes were originally inspired by the brush strokes of ancient Chinese scribes.

This is the oldest style of bonsai and was established long before it became popular in Japan. It is the original link between horticulture and art.

In nature this style is invariably limited to exposed, mountain conifers such as Scots pine, larch or spruce, which naturally shed lower branches as they mature. Very rarely does one find a literati deciduous tree of any beauty.

1 *We chose this Atlantic cedar because of the potential offered by the long, low branch.*

The essence of the design is the trunk line, which should have taper and should present many changes of direction. The branches are limited to the uppermost portion of the trunk and foliage is kept to a minimum – just sufficient to maintain the tree's health.

In this case we are using a garden centre cedar whose initial attraction was the long lower branch, which eventually becomes the leader. It is amazing how often the removal of most of the trunk, and the selection of a lower branch to take its place, can create ancient-looking and dramatic effects.

2 *The surface roots of this plant were buried deep in the pot. The net needs cutting away.*

3 *The obvious first step is to remove the unwanted upper trunk, leaving a stub to form a jin later. Using a branch as the new leader increases taper and creates a sharp bend.*

4 *Next the short spurs and tufts of foliage need to be cleaned from the trunk, and the first quarter of each branch. Then you can select which branches to keep and which to prune.*

6 *When shaping the trunk, aim for a combination of sharp bends and gradual curves. Try not to make them predictable, and remember to work in three dimensions, not two.*

7 *Tidy up the tree with scissors and then inspect the roots. Fortunately they are in excellent condition, as you can see.*

5 *The stub of the original trunk is jinned and the trunk and branches are wired.*

Left: *Three months later, the tree has put on considerable growth, and has already had its first pinching. As the tree develops, the bottom two (perhaps even four) branches will be removed!*

This knot of thick root could become an interesting feature

Final adjustments have been made to the shape of the trunk

The trunk has already swelled, so the wire must soon be replaced

GARDEN SHRUB: JUNIPER

As the name implies, this style is inspired by trees found growing on cliff-tops, where they are shaped by constant exposure to prevailing winds. Although the principles behind the design are simple, it can be difficult to arrive at a totally convincing result and much depends on the potential of the raw material.

The most suitable species for this style are conifers, since their foliage pads have cleaner outlines and their growth can be precisely controlled. With deciduous trees the larger leaves face all directions, ruining the effect, particularly on smaller bonsai.

Choose a plant which already has a tendency to grow towards one side, or has one side branch showing potential, which can become the main trunk. This will make the training that much easier.

Keep the trunk and the first half to two-thirds of the branch line completely clear of foliage. In nature winds not only shape the branches, they also strip young shoots and only allow new growth at the tips, where the force of the wind is broken by the rest of the tree.

This process must be imitated by the bonsai artist in the years that follow the initial styling. This will inevitably lead to over-extended growth, so every few years it will be necessary to cut the foliage pads back as far as possible and re-grow them. As a result you will create an ever more angular and battered looking branch structure which will add to the beauty of your bonsai.

1 *This Chinese juniper outgrew its space in a neighbour's rock garden. The root ball is wrapped in netting to keep it intact while we are working out the tree.*

Never be afraid to adjust the design as time passes by removing or jinning branches, or creating sharis on the trunk. The more 'damage' you can create on this style of bonsai, the more convincing it will eventually become. The essence of this design is to create a tree which looks as though it has been subjected to the worst the weather can throw at it over many years.

2 *From underneath the main trunk line is more visible. Start by removing all dead shoots and weak, spindly branches.*

3 *The trunkline is now clear, but there's more pruning to do yet. Windswept trees shed branches as they grow, retaining just a few on the lee side.*

4 *The unwanted branches have been removed and some of the thicker ones jinned. Now the tree is beginning to take shape. The smaller trunk on the right may come in useful later.*

5 *Having wired the remaining branches, they should all be shaped to follow the wind-blown sweep of the trunk.*

6 *All downward-facing shoots must now be cut off to emphasise the flowing branch lines, characteristic of the windswept style.*

Initial styling is complete. The secondary trunk has gone, as it conflicted with the overall design. Some jins have been shaped with heat (see page 123)*. From now on the branches will be allowed to extend to the left, without gaining in bulk.*

7 *Note how the foliage pads are being trimmed to a narrow wedge shape – another device to enhance the illusion of a tree which is subjected to strong prevailing winds.*

HOME-GROWN STOCK: SIBERIAN ELM

The tree featured on this spread is a Siberian elm grown from seed, which had been growing in open ground for six years before being potted up in early spring a year ago. Siberian Elm are vigorous trees and are ideal for this method of styling.

What we are doing here in effect is building a bonsai. We start by developing a good trunk with an interesting line and pronounced taper. The next step is to add the branches. As you can see we have plenty of choice. Many of the older branches are too thick to bend next to the trunk so we will concentrate on the young, thinner ones.

1 *Many of these branches are too thick. They would split away from the trunk when bent.*

The best time to tackle a project like this is in mid-summer, while the tree still has plenty of time to put on a lot more growth before autumn. If you do it too late in the year the new growth will not be fully hardened before the frosts begin and it will wither.

- When positioning the basic branch structure you should avoid straight lines (unless you are producing a formal upright style) and try to bend the branch at each point where a side shoot emerges. Remember to introduce vertical curves as well as horizontal ones.

- Feed the tree well to encourage new growth but reduce the nitrogen content towards late summer in order to harden off any tender young shoots.

- Allow all the new shoots which emerge from the branches to grow unchecked in order to thicken the host branches.

2 *After a couple of weeks the remaining shoots have recovered and put on some more growth. Only a few will be trained, the rest will go.*

- Apply the wire fairly loosely because the branches will thicken and set rapidly.

- Check the wiring after three weeks and then every few days after that. As soon as it appears too tight renew it immediately.

- Next spring the long shoots can be pruned back and selected ones wired into position to form the secondary branches. New growth from these should be allowed to extend to six or seven leaf nodes, and then trimmed back to two or three. These, too, can be loosely wired into position. Feeding heavily will mean that you will need to repeat this 'grow and clip' cycle several times throughout the season.

3 *Selected shoots are shortened and wired into position. Any over-long side shoots are also shortened to encourage bushy growth. Exaggerated curves will diminish later on.*

__Below:__ By the end of the season the foliage pads are developing well. I have changed the 'front', preferring the trunk line from this angle. Next spring I will plant the tree in a proper bonsai pot.

Training Ground

Finding a concealed corner of the garden for trees in various stages of training is far better than cluttering your display area with them. It is preferable to keep the display area free for those trees whose training has been completed and which you do not mind being seen. All sorts of temporary containers can be used on the training ground, from flower pots to my favourite – old plastic washing-up bowls. These are soft and malleable enough to adapt to your specific requirements. For example, drainage holes can be introduced in them by pushing a red hot pipe through the bottom of the bowl.

LANDSCAPE PLANT: SCOTS PINE

Most big garden centres, especially those who specialise in landscaping, will stock large container-grown trees and shrubs. These can offer tremendous potential and are, surprisingly, rather easier to work on than you may think at first.

Although Japanese pine bonsai are grown in many styles: literati, cascade, driftwood, etc., the vast majority of commercial trees seem to be stocky, thick-trunked uprights. These full triangular shapes are more reminiscent of young pine trees in the west. If you look at the pines in your neighbourhood you will discover they have a style all of their own, approaching literati sometimes, but relatively straight-trunked with cascading branches. This is the style we are aiming for here. This sort of operation can be carried out any time between early summer and early autumn.

1 *Pines always produce whorls of branches like these. Most should be pruned away.*

2 *If many branches are allowed to remain, they form thick 'knuckles' and disfigure the trunk. All but one or two branches should be pruned away. Here, most branches have been cut, leaving only those which are needed for the design. The front, which displays the best trunk shape, is marked with a pencil stuck in the pot.*

3 *The secondary trunk is positioned so it is visible from the front. All old needles are removed to make wiring easier and to encourage back budding before wiring the lower left branch.*

5 *Wires are not sufficient to hold the secondary trunk in place, so a tourniquet fixed to the pot's rim takes the strain.*

6 *Thick branches can be made to bend closer to the trunk by gently splitting them away.*

4 *The main branches are positioned to cascade gently from the trunks, and curves are introduced to the upper trunk. The original leader is removed and replaced with a smaller branch.*

7 *These fine white strands are mycelium of a mycorrhyzal fungus which helps the tree absorb nutrients from the soil. If you find this, keep it.*

8 *After more thinning, the secondary branches are wired into position.*

Above: *Stage one is complete. The pointed crown will be rounded off in time, and may even be lowered by pruning away the apex.*

Driftwood Style: Jins

One interpretation of the Japanese term *jin* is 'Godhead', but its definition in bonsai terms is rather less spiritual. Basically a jin is a dead branch which has shed its bark. In nature such branches are etched by the wind and rain and become bleached by the sun.

Jins are frequently seen on most old conifers and even on some deciduous trees, like oak.

By artificially creating jins on a bonsai you can impart a feeling of great age, and when done with care, their form and colour can complement the foliage masses to great effect. Get into the habit of creating jins every time you branch prune conifers, rather than removing the branch completely. If you don't like it after having lived with it for a while you can always cut it off later.

You can create jins at normal pruning time, but the best time is during the summer, when the bark is full of sap and is easier to strip and the wound will heal quickly.

Once you have made the jin you can give it texture by tearing the grain or by carving and sanding it to the desired shape. A jin will appear larger with a coarse texture than it would if given a smoother finish, so remember: the smaller the bonsai, the smoother the jin.

Another good point to bear in mind is that on a developing bonsai the foliage masses will grow, but the jins won't! If your new jins look too big now, they may well be in better proportion in a few year's time, so don't be too hasty in reducing their size at first.

1 *To create a jin, cut through the bark around the base of the branch. Then make another cut along its length. Make the cut 'eye shaped'.*

2 *Squeezing the bark with some flat-jawed pliers helps separate the bark from the wood.*

3 *The bark should peel away quite easily. If you are doing this in the autumn you may find the bark is a bit more stubborn.*

4 *A natural-looking shape and texture can be created by peeling back slivers of wood.*

5 *The shaped jin can be refined, and any fuzz removed, with fine sandpaper or a piece of glass, although don't sand it perfectly smooth.*

6 *In nature jins are bleached by the sun. In bonsai this effect is achieved by treating them with lime sulphur, which also preserves the wood.*

This overgrown Chinese juniper resembles a bush rather than a dignified tree.

BENDING JINS

1 *Branches on vigorous trees tend to grow straight, whereas a curved jin may well be better.*

2 *After a few minutes the heat will soften the resin, making the wood flexible.*

3 *Hold the jin in the desired position until it has cooled completely.*

Driftwood Style: Sharis

Sharis are related to jins but reflect a much more dramatic struggle with nature, causing a loss of bark from the trunk. This could be the result of lightning, disease, the battle with the elements, or it may just be the way the tree naturally ages.

Like jins, sharis are more appropriate on conifer bonsai, but for inspiration on deciduous trees take a look at our lowland pollarded willows with split trunks, or ancient hollow oaks.

The extreme use of sharis is employed in the creating of driftwood style bonsai. They are carved and refined to form wonderful shapes and textures which become more visually significant than the foliage masses. This is true living sculpture which represents the highest level of bonsai as an art form.

- It is best to take several seasons to create a big shari, stripping more bark each time.
- Bark is part of the tree's transport system, so always leave enough to support the foliage. On no account remove bark from immediately below a branch or it will die.
- Never allow a shari to encircle the trunk completely or the tree will die above that point.
- Junipers will live happily with a spiral of living bark, provided the shari is created gradually over several seasons. Pines will accept a gentle curve but spruces require a more or less straight line of living tissue from root to branch.
- Give the bonsai the proper aftercare by placing it in a lightly sheltered spot until all the remaining branches show new growth.

1 *Mark the outline of the shari with white paint before you cut. Make the line echo the shape of the trunk. Cut through to the wood.*

2 *If you do this in summer, when the sap is flowing, the bark will come away cleanly. The dark area is where the exposed wood of the original shari has weathered.*

Preserving

- Lime sulphur will help preserve the exposed wood as well as bleaching it, but one application lasts for only a short time. However, its effect is cumulative, so repeated twice-yearly applications will eventually almost 'fossilise' the wood.

- Very large areas of exposed wood may begin to decay at the base, where the trunk is constantly moist. These areas can be treated with clear horticultural preservative, a little at a time. But don't let any run off into the soil.

3 *Seal the edges of the shari with narrow strips of cut paste in order to prevent the cut surfaces from drying out.*

4 *Note how the shari and jins flow from one another. Also note how the shari runs from one side of the trunk to the other, enhancing the natural movement of the trunk line.*

5 *As with jins, the exposed wood must be treated with lime sulphur to preserve and bleach it. The old shari will blend with the new one after a couple of applications.*

Refining the Image

When fully refined and preened, ready for display, the bonsai image should appear almost as if it is frozen in time. Each branch should be perfectly positioned and clearly defined, with each neatly trimmed foliage pad floating in its own space.

As with all artistic disciplines, much depends on the aesthetic taste of the individual, but it is surprising how many experienced bonsai artists always seem to return to the classic Japanese principles, which have, after all, been developed over many years.

There is a grace and poise about classic Japanese bonsai, which can literally take your breath away. The ability to create a near-perfect image by using the minimum number of elements has taken many centuries to develop and refine, and will continue to set the standard for many years to come.

No bonsai is perfect, and the fact that all bonsai are living, growing plants means that they are constantly changing, requiring repeated attention to maintain their image. Even so, they can only look their best for a few weeks at a time, after which they will, again, gradually begin to outgrow their ideal form.

This tree has had its image refined for the first time, but there are still many faults in the design. Over the next five or six years it will go through similar processes many more times, hopefully improving on each occasion. Eventually it may reach the stage where I am totally satisfied with it.

Literati and Windswept

Below: By removing all branches apart from one, a fine literati style could be created. The shari has been extended and spiralled around the trunk, and a delicate, round pot is selected for the design.

Above: Equally dramatic, this wild windswept style involves changing the planting angle, and using a slab instead of a pot.

OTHER STYLES

Left: This shohin bonsai uses only the two lowest branches, which need several applications of wire before they can be positioned correctly. By removing the upper branches and turning the tree through 45 degrees **(right)**, a much more compact style evolves.

PREPARING FOR A DISPLAY

When bonsai are in a public show they come under very close scrutiny. It is essential that when your works of art are displayed they look their best. They should be sparkling with health and spotlessly clean.

All debris such as dead or discoloured leaves must be removed, and the surface of the soil must be free of weeds. The trunk and main branches will probably need cleaning, as will the pot.

It is very tempting to use bamboo or split cane as a backdrop to a display, but this is far too 'busy' and detracts attention from the trees. It is far better to use a pale, neutral coloured, untextured surface.

The same goes for the table, although woven reed matting can be used provided the trees are displayed on simple, low wooden stands. If you don't have suitable stands, you can construct some low boxes and paint them the same colour as the backdrop. The important thing is to keep it simple.

Keep labels small and the information basic. You only need to state the species (botanical and common names), the style and the age. The owner's or artist's name can also be included.

Also, remember that the public will love to touch your bonsai, so take whatever precautions you can to prevent this happening. It is not unknown for people to try and take cuttings from bonsai displays!

1 ***Below:*** *Study the outline of the tree carefully and snip off anything which breaks the periphery. A photograph often reveals faults the eye misses.*

2 *Pick out all weeds and dead moss, making sure to pull out all the roots as well. This is good general practice, even if you are not exhibiting.*

3 *You can make the surface more attractive by dressing it with fresh soil. Standard soil with extra grit generally looks very good.*

4 *Juniper trunks should have all the flaky bark brushed off with an old toothbrush. Stubborn bits of bark in awkward places can be rubbed off with sandpaper.*

5 *Once the bark has been removed the trunk can be given added colour by burnishing it with a soft, lint-free cloth, moistened with just a little vegetable oil.*

6 *Deciduous trees tend to accumulate green algae on their trunks and branches. Although some people like green trunks, algae should always be scrubbed off before exhibiting.*

7 *Glazed pots just need to be washed, but unglazed pots need to be rubbed down with wire wool or fine sandpaper to remove all the blemishes and lime scale.*

8 ***Right:*** *Additional patina can be given to the unglazed pots by rubbing the surface with a very slightly oily finger. Too much oil will make the surface too shiny and will ruin the effect.*

***Above:** This mixed display of bonsai won a Certificate of Special Merit at the National Exhibition. The stands are plain and simple; it is plain to see that all the effort went into the presentation of the trees themselves. This is a good basic tenet to keep in mind when you are exhibiting bonsai – it is the trees that people are interested in, not any paraphernalia that surrounds them.*

FURTHER INFORMATION

The main aim of bonsai is to create a tree-like form in miniature. This can be anything from a precise replica of a classic parkland beech to the image of a gnarled and weather-beaten mountain-top juniper, which can be almost abstract in its design.

***Above:** This magnificent display, modelled on an authentic Japanese bonsai garden, was mounted at the Chelsea Flower show by members of the British Bonsai Association.*

CLUBS

As you become more engrossed in bonsai, there will be occasions when you need first-hand advice. Your local nursery will be able to help diagnose health problems and may even offer a 'hospital' service. But when it comes to solving difficult design challenges or mastering techniques you can't seem to get the hang of, your best bet is to join a bonsai club. Any bonsai nursery will put you in touch with the nearest club. If there isn't one within easy reach you could consider starting one. Again, ask your nurseryman for the address of the national bonsai organisation, who will be glad to help and advise.

At each monthly meeting there is a table show of members' trees, a problem-solving session and a topic for the evening. This can range from a talk on choosing the right pot or a slide show of a famous collection, to a demonstration by a visiting master of an

***Right:** This group of English elms was inspired by the hilltop copses of the Berkshire Downs, before they were devastated by Dutch elm disease in the late 1970s.*

advanced new technique. No matter how experienced you are, you will always leave a meeting knowing more.

WORKSHOPS

Many clubs and nurseries organise workshops for small numbers of people, where students work on their own material under the guidance of a teacher. These affairs usually last all day and are by far the best way to learn. In many cases it is possible to go along just to watch, but you don't benefit nearly as much as you do by taking part yourself.

EXHIBITIONS

Every year there are several bonsai exhibitions around the country. Studying top-class bonsai at your leisure can be extremely rewarding. You will learn a lot from discovering how others have shaped their trees, and by seeing the result of techniques you have yet to try. Take heart from the fact that many of these specimen bonsai are created from native stock by people who were themselves beginners not long ago.

CONVENTIONS

Many countries hold annual or bi-annual conventions, which take place over a three-day weekend. These include exhibitions, demonstrations by international masters, workshops and visits to famous collections. There are sales areas offering everything from seeds to specimen bonsai, as well as every accessory imaginable. They attract a large number of enthusiasts from overseas and many firm friendships have been struck at such events.

Every four years a different country hosts the World Convention sponsored by the World Bonsai Friendship Federation, which was inaugurated at the first such event in Omiya, Japan in 1989. This is bonsai heaven, where you can meet top bonsai artists from all over the world who are always happy to pass the benefit of their experience to anyone who cares enough to ask.

You don't have to be an expert to attend an international bonsai convention, so don't be put off from going. The only qualification necessary is enthusiasm. And when it's over, and you are on your way home, you will remember when you planted your first seedling in a shallow pot. You will wonder how you could ever have imagined that such a simple act could lead to a whole new world of excitement and challenge, friendship and artistic fulfilment.

Above: *A colleague of Masahiko Kimura, pioneer of the 'new wave' of bonsai artists, instructing a nervous English student at the European convention in Turin, Italy.*

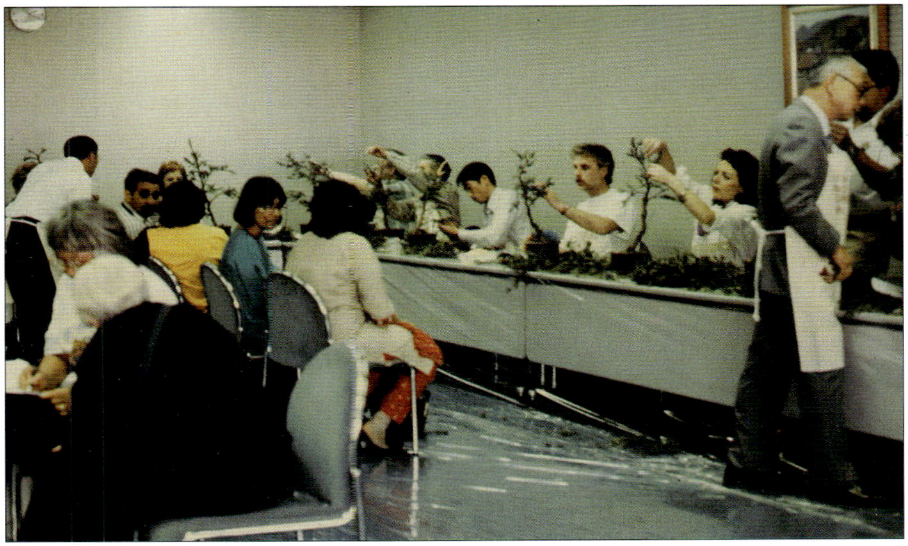

Above: *A silent audience watches respectfully as students work on literati-style bonsai under the guidance of the Japanese master, Tom Yamamoto.*

GLOSSARY

This list contains botanical and horticultural terms relevant to bonsai as well as terms unique to bonsai.

ABCISSION LAYER The layer of cork which forms at the base of the petiole on deciduous trees in autumn. This layer creates a seal preventing the flow of nutrients, causing the leaf to fall.

ACID Describes soil with a pH of less than 7.0. Although most trees will grow happily in acid soils, some, including field maple and beech, do better in alkaline conditions.

ADVENTITIOUS A term applied to shoots arising from parts of the plant other than the growing points, usually on older wood such as trunk or wound scars.

ALKALINE Describes soils with a pH of over 7.0, or rich in lime. Most trees will grow in alkaline soil, but others, notably azaleas, require acid conditions to survive. Alkalinity can be corrected by using any of the commercial soil acidifiers.

ALTERNATE Refers to leaves which appear singly, first on one side of the shoot, and then on the other.

APEX The tip of a shoot, or a tree, from which extension growth takes place. In bonsai this point is dictated by aesthetic considerations and is not necessarily the focus of the tree's energy.

APICAL Describes a shoot at the tip of a branch or a bud at the tip of a shoot.

AXIL, AXILLARY The angle between a leaf and its parent shoot, which always contains at least one bud. Also the angle between a vein and the midrib of a leaf.

BANKAN Bonsai style. A tree with a twisted or coiled trunk.

BARK A protective layer covering trunk and branches, consisting of living corky cells on the inside, generated annually by the cambium, and dead cells on the outside.

BASAL Applies to fresh growth arising from the base of a plant.

BLEEDING The excessive loss of sap from new wounds, often the plant's natural device to prevent infection entering the wound.

BLIND Describes a shoot which has failed to develop an apical bud.

BOLE The clear trunk of a tree, from ground level to the lowest branch.

BROADLEAVED Denotes any tree which is not a conifer.

BUD A tightly condensed embryonic shoot, usually protected by scales formed by modified leaves.

BUNJINGI Bonsai style (Literati). Originating in China during the T'ang dynasty, and reflecting calligraphic brush-strokes.

CALCIFUGE A plant which cannot tolerate alkaline soil.

CALLUS The 'scar' tissue, generated by the cambium, which forms over a wound or at the base of a cutting prior to root initiation.

CAMBIUM The thin growing layer between the bark and the wood which is responsible for laying down new bark on the outside and new wood on the inside each growing season, increasing the girth of the trunk. The cambium layer also forms new roots on cuttings, new buds, and graft unions.

CANOPY The foliage-bearing upper and outer reaches of a tree.

CHLOROPHYLL The natural green substance in plants, whose function is to convert carbon dioxide from the air, and water from the soil, into carbohydrates, using sunlight as a catalyst (photosynthesis).

CHOKKAN Bonsai style (Formal upright). A straight, unbroken trunk, persisting to the tree's apex, with symmetrically arranged branches.

COLLAR The swelling at the point of union between a branch and the trunk.

COMPOST 1: Partially decayed vegetable matter. 2: A mixture of sand, humus and other ingredients used as a growing medium.

COMPOUND Describes a leaf which is made up of a number of leaflets, attached to a central rib.

CONIFER A cone-bearing tree, usually with needle-like leaves.

COTYLEDON The first leaves to emerge from a seed, usually thick and fleshy, and unlike the true leaves.

CROWN The upper part of a tree formed by the branches and upper trunk.

CUTICLE A waxy coating on a leaf which reduces moisture loss and helps to prevent damage by external factors such as frost.

CUTTING A section of stem, root or leaf which is taken for propagation.

DAMPING-OFF A fungal disease causing seedlings to collapse during the first few weeks after germination.

DECIDUOUS A tree or shrub which sheds its leaves each autumn.

DEFOLIATION Natural shedding or artificial removal of leaves.

DENDROLOGY The study of trees.

DIE-BACK The withering and death of shoots or branches due to disease, drought or some other adverse condition.

DORMANT 1: Describes a bud which did not produce growth during the season following its formation, but which retains the ability to produce growth in the future. 2: The resting period during autumn and winter when the tree puts on little or no growth.

DRAWN Refers to plants which have grown uncharacteristically tall and slender due to overcrowding or poor light.

DWARF A genetic mutation of a species producing a small, compact growth habit.

EPICORMIC A term referring to growth emerging from dormant buds.

EVERGREEN A tree or shrub which bears foliage throughout the year.

EXOTIC A plant originating from another country, regardless of climate or location.

EYE An undeveloped bud on a shoot over one year old.

FERTILISER A substance which provides one or more essential plant nutrients.

FLUSH A surge of new growth. Most trees produce one flush in spring and another in mid-summer.

FORCING Accelerating the growth or

development of a plant by artificially changing its growing conditions.

FUKINAGASHI Bonsai style (Windswept). Depicting a tree exposed to strong prevailing winds.

GALL An abnormal growth on a root, stem or leaf, caused by a microscopic insect.

GENUS A group of related species.

GIRTH The circumference of the trunk of a tree, measured at chest height in full size specimens.

GO-KAN Bonsai style – five trunked.

GRAFTING The vegetative bonding of one part of a plant to another.

HABIT The natural shape or growth pattern of a plant.

HABITAT The conditions and location in which a plant is normally found in nature.

HAN-KENGAI Bonsai style (Semi-cascade). The apex must fall below the rim of the pot but not below its base.

HALF-HARDY Describes a plant which can tolerate cold but not sub-zero temperatures.

HARDENING-OFF The process of gradually introducing a plant grown under protection to outside conditions.

HARDWOOD The term used for timber from broadleaved trees.

HARDY Describes a plant which can survive outside during winter.

HOKIDACHI Bonsai style (Broom). All branches emerge from the same point at the top of a short, straight trunk.

HUKMUS Partially decayed organic matter present in the soil.

IKADABUKI Bonsai style (Raft). The plant is laid on its side and the branches are trained vertically to form many trunks.

INORGANIC Applies to any chemical compound which does not contain carbon. In horticulture the term describes manufactured fertilisers, growing mediums and treatments.

INTERNODE The distance between the leaf nodes on a shoot.

ISHITSUKI Bonsai style (Root on rock) A rock replaces the pot.

JIN A branch or trunk apex which has been stripped of its bark, shaped, bleached and preserved.

JOHN INNES A series of basic compost recipes containing sand, humus, loam and fertiliser.

JUVENILE Refers to foliage produced during stages of rapid growth, which is distinct from adult foliage.

KABUDACHI Bonsai style (Clump). Several trunks arising from the same point on a root.

KENGAI Bonsai style (Cascade). The apex is below the pot's base.

KYONAL Proprietary Japanese wound sealant for bonsai.

LATERAL A shoot emerging from a bud on a main stem.

LAYERING A means of propagating from mature growth by removing bark to encourage adventitious root growth to emerge from above the wound.

LEACHING The process by which nutrients and minerals are washed out of the soil by the passage of water.

LEADER The dominant shoot.

LENTICEL A pore on a shoot or stem of a tree.

LIME Calcium as a soil constituent.

LIME SULPHUR Originally used as an insecticide and fungicide, the compound is now used to preserve and bleach jins and sharis.

LOAM Normal, good garden soil.

MAME Miniature bonsai, able to 'sit comfortably in the palm of a hand'.

MOYOGI Bonsai style (Informal upright). The trunk consists of a series of curves with symmetrically arranged branches.

NEAGARI Bonsai style (Exposed root).

NEBARI The exposed surface roots.

NETSUNANARI Bonsai style (Root connected). Several trunks arising from different points on the same root system.

NODE A stem joint or the point at which a leaf or leaves are attached to the stem.

OPPOSITE The arrangement of leaves in pairs on either side of the shoot.

ORGANIC Any chemical compound containing carbon. In horticulture the term refers to any compound or growing medium which is not manufactured or synthetic.

PEAT Sphagnum moss or sedge in an arrested state of decay, caused by lack of oxygen in its natural, waterlogged habitat.

PETIOLE The stalk of a leaf.
pH A unit of measuring the acid/alkaline balance of a soil.

PHOTOSYNTHESIS The process by which a plant manufactures sugars by utilising light and chlorophyll to combine carbon dioxide and water Vital to plant life.

ROOT HAIRS Single cell projections from the root responsible for absorbing water and nutrients from the soil.

SABAMIKI Bonsai style (Driftwood). The major part of the trunk consists of a shari.

SANKAN Bonsai style (Three trunks).

SAPWOOD The living tissues forming the layers of wood immediately beneath the bark.

SEKIJÔJU Bonsai style (Root over rock).

SHAKAN Bonsai style (Slanting).

SHARI The portion of a trunk which has had the bark removed and has been bleached.

STOMATA The breathing pores on leaves.

SUCKER A new shoot arising from the roots of an established tree.

TAP ROOT The main downward-growing root of a plant or young tree.

TENDER Describes a plant which cannot tolerate low temperatures.

TERMINAL Refers to the upper shoot, flower or bud.

TRANSPIRATION The continual passage of water vapour through pores on leaves and stems.

VEGETATIVE Describes propagation by any means other than by seed.

YOSE-UE Bonsai style (Group or multi-trunked).

ZELKOVA Japanese grey bark elm used extensively to create one of the newest bonsai styles – the broom style.

INDEX

This index lists all the bonsai species, styles and techniques mentioned in this book. It also comprises entries for essential tools, materials and important ancillary information. For a general guide to the book, see the list of contents on page 9. For an explanation of terms, see the glossary on pages 134–7.

W, Y, Z

ACKNOWLEDGEMENTS

I am particularly grateful to my friends Peter Chan, of Herons Nursery, and Ruth Stafford-Jones, for allowing us to photograph trees from their private collections, and Bill Jordan for his advice and the loan of his photographs of pests and diseases. Thanks are also due to China's Bonsai, for the loan of their workshop, to Sally Strugnell for her excellent design, and to Neil Sutherland for his enthusiasm and endless patience behind the camera.

A bonsai is a work of art, whose beauty is entirely dependent upon the skills of its current caretaker. It is therefore important to record who is responsible for the beauty of the specimen bonsai pictured in this book.

Ruth Stafford–Jones: Pages 18, 23, 27, 78, 87
Peter Chan: pages: 16, 21, 50, 56, 59, 65, 73, 77, 87, 93, 95, 96, 98, 104, 107, 111

All the other trees are from my own collection.